MUSTANG

MUSTANG

JIM CAMPISANO

MetroBooks

An Imprint of Friedman/Fairfax Publishers

© 1997 by Michael Friedman Publishing Group, Inc.

Library of Congress Cataloging-in-Publication Data available
upon request.

ISBN 1-56799-438-5

Editors: Carrie Chase and Stephen Slaybaugh
Art Director: Kevin Ullrich
Photography Editor: Karen L. Barr
Production Manager: Jeanne Hutter

Color separations by HK Scanner Arts Int'l Ltd.
Printed and bound in China by Leefung-Asco Printers Ltd.

10 9 8 7 6 5 4 3 2 1

For bulk purchases and special sales, please contact:
Friedman/Fairfax Publishers
Attention: Sales Department
15 West 26th Street
New York, NY 10010
212/685-6610   FAX 212/685-1307

Visit our website:
http://www.metrobooks.com

DEDICATION

For Donna, my partner and greatest inspiration.

ACKNOWLEDGMENTS

Special thanks to O. John Coletti and the rest of the hardcore Mustang lovers at the Ford Motor Company for keeping the fire burning even when others tried to extinguish it. Also, my gratitude goes out to Tom Corcoran for the extra set of eyes and to my staff at *Muscle Mustangs & Fast Fords* for their tireless efforts to expand the high-performance universe.

CONTENTS

INTRODUCTION 8

CHAPTER ONE 1965–1966 OVERNIGHT SENSATION 10

CHAPTER TWO 1967–1968 THE PONY GROWS UP 26

CHAPTER THREE 1969–1970 A THOROUGHBRED AT LAST 42

CHAPTER FOUR 1971–1973 THE END OF THE LINE 56

CHAPTER FIVE 1974–1978 SCORE MUSTANG II, PERFORMANCE 0 66

CHAPTER SIX 1979–1986 FOX ON THE RUN 74

CHAPTER SEVEN 1987–1993 LONG LIVE THE KING 90

CHAPTER EIGHT 1994–1996 GALLOPING INTO THE TWENTY-FIRST CENTURY 102

APPENDICES 116

INDEX 118

INTRODUCTION

You're alone on a desert road. The sun is setting and you are miles from the nearest house. There isn't another car in sight. You press the accelerator pedal to the floor and the powerful Ford V8 presses you into the bucket seat. Soon the speedometer needle has passed 100 mph... 120... 140... This is what the Ford Mustang is all about.

You're cruising South Beach in Miami. It's January and the top on your '65 convertible is down. You are barely moving because of the traffic, but that's okay. While people in other parts of the country are freezing, you're listening to your favorite tunes while warm ocean breezes blow through your hair. Gawkers from the chic sidewalk restaurants stare admiringly at you and your machine. This is what the Mustang is all about.

Maybe your last child just graduated from college and a new six-cylinder model is in your driveway. After spending the last two decades behind the wheels of assorted station wagons and minivans, this is what you've rewarded yourself with—a candy-apple–colored machine that will carry you and your golf clubs to your next tee-off. This, too, is what the Mustang is all about.

Never has one car been so many different things to so many different types of people. For some, the Mustang is a brutish race car, barely streetable—if at all—and for more than 30 years, young people have braved hellish insurance rates and outlandish fuel prices for the opportunity to own their version of America's most popular sporty car.

At the same time, the Mustang has been embraced from Day One (April 17, 1964) by millions of people who ordinarily couldn't care less what they drive, so long as it gets them where they need to be reliably. It has been said that the Mustang was magical. The old became young again, the ordinary seemed glamorous, and with a base price of under $2,500 in '64, even the poor could afford a piece of the American dream. The Mustang has been

Base price for the Shelby GT350 convertible in 1969 was still under $4,800, excellent for a striking, low-volume performance car, but still nearly $2,000 more than a base Mustang convertible.

bought by celebrities—Sonny and Cher each had one in '65, as did Frank Sinatra; singer Jim Morrison of the Doors terrorized the streets in a Shelby GT500—and common folk alike. It even became somewhat of a celebrity itself, starring in films such as *Goldfinger, Bullitt,* and *Bull Durham.*

While some scoffed at its plebeian roots (the Mustang shared its platform with the Falcon, Ford's low-dollar compact), there was a purity in its design and a free-spiritedness in its demeanor that attracted buyers like no car before it. Best of all, it had the longest option list in the industry—order the right equipment and it was akin to buying a custom car straight from the dealer. It could be anything from a low-buck commuter car with a six-cylinder engine and three-speed manual transmission to an all-out race car with a high-output V8, competition suspension, and four-on-the-floor tranny.

Not only was the Mustang a good car, but it was also the right automobile for the right time. The first wave of America's 78 million baby boomers had just reached driving age around the time of the Mustang's introduction. The muscle car era, which began around 1960, was in full swing and Ford would soon be offering Mustangs with some of the hairiest power plants imaginable. Perhaps most important of all, women began driving in increasingly large numbers. Unlike most of Detroit's offerings of that era, the Mustang was not the size of a house. It was small, easily maneuverable, cute to some, and sexy to others. From the very beginning, women accounted for nearly one-quarter of all Mustang sales—an unprecedented phenomenon.

From the moment Mustang mania started, its owners have been among the most loyal. It is believed that some 472 Mustang-only clubs sprang up in the car's first three years of existence and the list of Mustang clubs worldwide still tops 450. As this is being written, plans are being made to open a national Mustang museum.

My personal Mustang roots run deep and are quite varied. My older brother had a 1966 coupe with a six-cylinder engine and a three-speed stick. Through a contest, my mother won the use of a '67 Shelby GT500 for a couple of weeks—just what she needed: 355 horsepower, a four-speed transmission, and a heavy-duty clutch. When I was in high school, a buddy of mine had a '71 Mach 1 with a nitrous-oxide injected 429 Super Cobra Jet. There was no excuse for being late for class when he was behind the wheel.

Somehow, first generation Mustangs have managed to elude me. There was a red '65 fastback that first illustrated why Mustangs had the nickname "Rustangs" and later a '67 convertible. They both had enough holes to fill the Albert Hall; I passed. I'm still looking for a '69 Mach 1, preferably a blue or black one with the 428 Cobra Jet and Shaker hood.

Today, my days are filled with late-model fuel-injected 5.0 Mustangs. As the editor of *Muscle Mustangs & Fast Fords* magazine, I have the pleasure of photographing, writing about, driving, and racing some of the fastest, most beautiful cars I've ever dreamed of. The Mustang of today proves that the car's original spirit is alive and well. The 5.0 Mustang is the car of choice among today's youth; it's the '55 Chevy for an entire new generation of Americans.

Over the years, the Mustang has spawned a host of imitators, both from domestic manufacturers and from Japan. It has also had its shares of ups and downs. But only the Mustang has appealed to such a wide audience—grandparents and their grandkids, men and women, cops and outlaws, car-people, and those who wouldn't know a dipstick from a hubcap. While it is slightly larger and definitely more expensive, the Mustang today remains true to its roots. It still delivers style, performance, fun, and romance at a price that is more or less affordable to the general public.

How many other cars can say that?

In their place was a single flamboyant stripe that was almost as wide as the grille and ran the length of the car, up the front bumper, down the hood, across the roof, and down the deck lid and spoiler to the bumper. Instead of the relatively thin matching stripe that ran down the side rocker moldings, an extra-wide stripe covered the front fender.

CHAPTER ONE

1965–1966
OVERNIGHT SENSATION

Perhaps it was the most calculated and carefully planned blitz since the Normandy invasion of World War II. Ford had purchased a solid block of advertising time on all three major television networks from 9:30 to 10:00 on the evening of April 16, 1964. With this unprecedented move, Ford introduced its new baby, the Mustang, to the American public.

The very next day, Ford unveiled the Mustang at no less a venue than the New York World's Fair.

The response was nothing short of amazing. So wildly enthusiastic was the reaction that there were virtual stampedes at Ford dealerships. An incredible 22,000 orders for the car were taken the first day. It met its first-year sales target of 100,000 units within four months. Inside of twelve months, more than 417,000 of Ford's "sporty car" were on the road. By comparison, when the Ford Taurus became the best-selling car in America in the 1990s, it was selling in the neighborhood of 350,000 units annually.

Mustang mania had taken America by storm, the same way Beatlemania had done just a few months earlier. How crazy did it get?

• A truck driver was so mesmerized by the sight of the new Mustang that he drove his truck through the dealership window.

• In Garland, Texas, fifteen people bid on the same Mustang, and the winner insisted on sleeping in the car

Though the Mustang was introduced in coupe and convertible form in April 1964, the fastback "2+2" model pictured here wasn't available until September of that year, when Ford's 1965 models hit the showrooms. All Mustangs built to this point were registered as 1965 models, but some people refer to the early cars today as '64½s. This '65 has the desirable V8 option, as indicated by the emblem at the leading edge of the front fender, as well as the styled steel wheels, which added $119.71 to the purchase price.

overnight to guarantee that it wouldn't get sold out from under him before his check cleared the following day.

• A Chicago dealer closed early and called the police when Mustang-crazed buyers overran the dealership.

• Parents bought 93,000 Mustang pedal cars for their children during the 1964 Christmas season.

No other car has provoked this kind of automotive frenzy. Ford may not have expected such an overwhelming response; however, the wild success didn't stop the company from fueling the fire further. It launched an enormous publicity campaign with print ads that compared the Mustang with exciting European sports cars, but with American value, practicality, and reliability.

"THE UNEXPECTED...MUSTANG HITS THE STARTING LINE FULL BORE!"

So said the ad in the June 1964 issue of *Hot Rod* magazine, which touted the car's three available V8 engines (including the high-winding 271-horsepower 289), its long list of optional features, and rock-solid dependability. If that weren't enough, a potential customer could send in $1 and get a "precisely detailed, authentic scale model of the new Ford Mustang."

Even in the notoriously conservative halls of Ford Motor Company, the accountants were dancing in the aisles. Here was a car that cost a relatively low $75 million to bring to market, and the factories couldn't build them fast enough. Plus, no one ordered a base Mustang. The many available options proved irresistible to the customers—and very profitable to Ford.

A Market in Search of a Car

So what exactly was the appeal? Why was the Mustang such a smash? The answers to these questions are fairly simple, but require some background.

By the time the Mustang was introduced, Ford had been touting the car's high performance and racing activities in its "Total Performance" ad campaign for over a year and was firmly entrenched in the horsepower war that had broken out between the Big Three automakers around 1955. Despite the fact that Ford cars were capturing checkered flags all over the globe in NASCAR stock-car racing, drag racing, Indy, and Grand Prix racing, this success was not translating into showroom sales.

For decades, Fords were notorious as the "hot cars" on the street. Their valve-in-block flathead V8s, first introduced in the 1932 model year, brought eight-cylinder performance to the masses. Previously, V8s were reserved for upscale, high-priced vehicles like Cadillacs and Packards while the working class puttered along in four-cylinder and six-cylinder Fords and Chevys. With the introduction of the 221 V8, Ford brought excitement where there had been none. Eventually, hot-rodders, tinkerers, and racers discovered that this little workhorse took to modifications the way a politician responds to graft, and for the next twenty years, every hot rod in the nation worth its salt was flathead-powered.

When Ford retired the flattie in 1953, it replaced it with the Y-block V8, so called for its deep-skirted engine block. This engine would turn out to be a dud, but it did fairly well in racing and in 1955 found a home in what is arguably the most beautiful Ford of the postwar era, the two-seat Thunderbird. Launched as an upscale alternative to Chevrolet's primitive (at the time) Corvette, it had enough good things going for it that it blew the fiberglass-bodied Chevy away in the sales department. For a

Chevrolet's Corvette was anything but an overnight sensation. Even the introduction of its new V8 engine in 1955 did little for sales—only 700 cars were produced that year, including this Sportsman Red model. The 265-cubic-inch engine made 195 horsepower and variations of it powered the Corvette until 1996. This was the Thunderbird's main competitor from 1955 to 1957.

time, in fact, the T-bird did very well in actual racing competition against the Vette, too.

The Thunderbird was a far more traditional automobile than its rival from Chevrolet. For starters, it had a steel body; roll-up windows instead of plastic side curtains; and a top that was easy to lower and raise. Its body was made by the Budd company, which was also in the business of making streamlined freight-train cars. The steel gave the Ford a huge edge over the Corvette, the body of which was somewhat flimsy. Fiberglass technology for automobile applications was still in its infancy, nowhere near as advanced as it is today although even today steel holds many advantages over fiberglass. The early Corvettes (1953–1955) were considered something of a novelty, whereas the Thunderbird was taken more seriously by car buyers. In its first season, it ridiculously outsold the Corvette—16,155 to 700.

After three years, 53,166 two-seat T-birds had been built, but Ford thought there was a larger market to be tapped. By adding a backseat and acres of sheet metal, Ford created the first "personal luxury" car. While it did not have the attractive, pure design of the two-seater, the four-seat "Square Bird"—so called because of its boxy design—proved to be much more popular. Ford moved 37,892 Thunderbirds in 1958, almost twice as many as in 1957. In 1959, this number nearly doubled again, to 67,456 units. While purists might have cringed, it was obvious that Ford's product planners had done their homework.

The only downside to the Thunderbird's newfound sales success was that it left Ford without a legitimate performance car. By 1957, the Corvette had matured. Thanks to a redesign in 1956—which gave it a roll-up window and an easier-to-operate top—and the introduction of fuel injection and a four-speed transmission the following year, the Vette started attracting a loyal following that

The 1957 Thunderbird was the last of the two-seaters. A 300-horsepower supercharged 312 V8 was available, but found few takers. Far more common were the standard engine, a 245-horse version of the 312, and a 270-horse version with twin four-barrel carbs.

continues to grow to this day. While it wasn't moving in Thunderbird-like numbers, it captured the hearts of performance enthusiasts, particularly young ones. On top of this, many of the Corvette's hot engines, including the powerful "fuelies," could be ordered in the full-size Chevrolets, dubbed the "Hot Ones" in ads.

Concurrently, the Y-block engine started earning a well-deserved reputation for sluggish performance and poor reliability. By the end of the fifties, Ford had lost its core support: the youth market.

This couldn't have come at a worse time. In the late fifties and early sixties, tens of millions of baby boomers were getting their driver's licenses and spending their money at Chevrolet dealerships on spiced-up Corvettes and Impalas, instead of T-Birds.

LET'S GET SMALL

The turn of the decade also saw the rise of the compact car in North America. Spurred on by the success of the Volkswagen Beetle, Ford, General Motors, and Chrysler each introduced a competitor to the German import in 1960. Ford's Falcon was the most conventional, looking for all the world like a downsized version of one of the company's full-size offerings. It was also conventional under the hood and in the interior as well, being powered by a sturdy six-cylinder engine up front and fitted with a traditional bench seat.

Dodge's Lancer and Plymouth's Valiant had normal six-cylinder engines, but their styling was very far out. While some called it "European," the buying public simply called it "ugly" and tended to avoid it.

Most radical was Chevrolet's Corvair, which, like the VW, had a rear-mounted, air-cooled engine, and unusual but very pleasing styling.

Though the Falcon sold better, Chevrolet began marketing a version of the Corvair known as the Monza, which came with such interesting, youth-targeted touches as bucket seats and a floor-mounted shifter—items that most people take for granted today, but were rather eccentric in American cars of the early sixties. The Monza caught on with its target audience, and although it was a late addition to the 1960 model lineup, it nevertheless sold 11,926 copies. In 1961, Chevrolet moved almost 110,000 Monzas. The following year, it created the Corvair Monza Spyder by adding a turbocharger to the flat six-cylinder engine. This was long before Ralph Nader wrote the book *Unsafe at Any Speed*, which virtually called the Corvair a death trap. Sales on the odd little Chevy were moving very briskly, and people in Dearborn were starting to take notice.

One of these people was a young executive named Lee Iacocca. He recognized early on that the demise of the two-seat Thunderbird left a gaping hole in the Ford model lineup. Iacocca understood that the youth market was about to explode; he also knew the impact that an exciting sports car could have on a company. But he was wise enough to realize that the market for genuine two-place automobiles was terribly limited. In its best year, the two-seat T-bird barely sold 21,000 copies, and it took until 1960 for the Corvette to exceed the 10,000-unit mark.

Chevrolet's economical rear-engined Corvair (above) was proving popular with young buyers thanks to its low price and options like bucket seats and floor-mounted shifters. The '65 Mustang (right), however, made the Corvair seem dowdy, especially when equipped with a sporty GT package and the High-Performance 289 engine.

But what if you designed a four-place automobile that was small enough and sporty enough to look like a two-seater? This was the idea that Iacocca and his cohorts in the now famous "Fairlane Committee"—named after the hotel where they held their meetings to discuss such a car—came up with.

Today, some thirty-plus years and 6.5 million or so Mustangs later, anyone can use 20-20 hindsight and say, "What a wonderful idea!" In 1962, though, Ford was still fresh off the Edsel disaster, a flop in the marketplace that cost the company hundreds of millions of dollars—even after the company had done more market research than it had for any other vehicle in its history. The Edsel was supposed to be a "can't fail" deal. Compared with it, the idea for what became the Mustang bordered on the radical. It was up to Iacocca to sell it to the brass.

Fortunately for the legions of Mustang lovers around the globe, Iacocca was (and to some degree, still is) a masterful salesman. He had risen through the Ford ranks from the bottom rung on the corporate ladder to become the youngest vice president in company history. In the sports business, he would have been known as "a natural." Still, had he not been able to bring the Mustang to market for relatively little money, it more than likely would have been stillborn. In 1961 or 1962, it took $300 million to $400 million to bring a totally new car to market. Following the Edsel fiasco, there was no chance that Ford was going to, dare we say, pony up that kind of capital on a risky prospect like the Mustang. This dictated that the car be built on the existing Falcon platform. By doing this, it brought the introduction cost down to a more reasonable $75 million.

(An interesting note: when Ford redesigned the Mustang in 1994 on its existing chassis, it spent some $700 million. Talk about inflation.)

If the Edsel was the most market-researched car in history, then the Mustang must have been the least so. But what little information the Fairlane Committee had garnered was convincing. According to *The Ford Mustang*, published by the public affairs department of the Ford Motor Company, car buyers aged eighteen to thirty-four were expected to account for more than 50 percent of the increase in new automobile sales projected for the coming decade.

SETTING THE PACE

As part of the Mustang's marketing program, it was named the official pace car for the forty-eighth annual Indianapolis 500. Knowing this spectacle would draw worldwide attention, Ford outfitted thirty-six vehicles in Pace Car garb. In this case, that meant special white paint (dubbed "Pace Car White") with blue stripes and the requisite "Indianapolis 500 Pace Car" decals on the side. While they all started life as 260 two-barrel models with automatic transmissions, three were pulled for actual race duty and fitted with specially prepared 289 engines and Borg-Warner T-10 transmissions. The engines had balanced bottom ends, high-performance hydraulic-lifter camshafts, reworked cylinder heads, and four-barrel carburetors.

To prepare the three ponies for the rigors of actually pacing the race, the suspensions were upgraded and fitted with beefier Firestone tires.

The thirty-three parade lap cars returned to dealer inventory fleets, while the three actual pace cars went to private owners. As per tradition, the actual car that started the race was given to that year's winner, A. J. Foyt. Legend has it that Foyt's secretary totaled the car shortly thereafter, and there is no documented evidence of what became of the two other specially prepped ragtops—though it is believed that one may be in Florida.

The Mustang has been the pace car for the Indianapolis 500 three times, in 1964, 1979, and 1994. Only 36 Pace Cars were built in '64 and the one that actually started the event (shown here with Harlan Fengler) was given to race winner A.J. Foyt.

IS IT A 1964 OR 1965?

While many enthusiasts refer to their early 1965 Mustangs as '64½ models, and Mustangs were, indeed, first sold during the latter part of the 1964 model year, the term "'64½" is actually technically incorrect. Mustangs built during the 1964 model year (before August 17, 1964) were registered as 1965 vehicles and should be referred to as either "early '65s" or, more simply, just "'65s." Mustangs built after August 17 are "late '65s."

What's the difference? Early '65s had different engines from those of the late '65s, different electrical systems, and certain trim oddities. All early '65s were equipped with generators, while late '65s had more modern alternators. Early '65s were powered by the 170 c.i. six-cylinder engine, the 164-hp 260 V8, and the 210-hp 289 V8, while late '65s got the 200-cube six-banger, plus 200- and 225-hp 289s. The only carryover engine was the high-performance (271-horsepower) 289, introduced in June 1964.

On early '65s, the passenger bucket seat was stationary, and it could be moved fore and aft on late '65s. Also, the shift handle on automatic transmission–equipped cars was smaller on early '65s.

On the long list of available options for the late '65s were the Rally Pac gauges mounted on the steering column and under-dash "knee-knocker" air conditioning.

Also, 36 percent of all persons under twenty-five liked the idea of "four on the floor"–style transmissions. Young people heavily favored bucket seats, with a survey of college students finding that 42 percent preferred them for first dates. Other preferences included the sound of a high-performance engine and the feeling of being close to the road.

Perhaps most important, market research showed that the number of multiple-car families was increasing rapidly. The driver of that second car was often female, someone who, studies revealed, wanted something small and easily maneuverable, but with personality.

The creation of the Mustang seems to have been one of the first times that the Big Three actually took female drivers into account when designing a car, and it paid off—about 25 percent of the first-generation cars were purchased by women.

To ensure that the "personality" that women wanted made it to the car, the job of styling the as-yet-unnamed Mustang went to Eugene Bordinat, vice president and director of styling; Joseph Oros, the chief stylist of Ford's exterior styling studio; and executive stylist of Ford's exterior studio Dave Ash. The job that this team did was nothing short of spectacular, and the importance of the car's styling cannot be underestimated. Today, people's top concerns in buying a new car seem to be price, fuel economy, and safety; in the sixties, sizzle sold cars. And while this may seem superficial, the original Mustang was simply terrific to look at. It had the appearance of a sports car, but had a backseat. It was small like a sports car, but not temperamental and impractical like the European MGs and Triumphs, automobiles that were infamous for not starting and for leaking oil.

The Mustang's list of virtues was long: it was inexpensive, with a base six-cylinder hardtop priced at a paltry $2,320.96, compared with $3,300 for a V8 Dart GT (a full-size Ford started at about $3,000); it possessed the reliability of an anvil, thanks in large part to its simple OHV 170-inch six-cylinder and small-block V8 engines; its standard bucket seats, floor shifters, and racy appearance made it exciting inside and out; and it was economical to drive and maintain.

One of the Mustang's most endearing traits was that it was a blast to drive, especially if you ordered one with the K-code 271-hp High-Performance 289, four-speed trans-

MUSTANG I AND MUSTANG II

The first Ford to bear the "Mustang" name in the 1960s was the two-seat experimental sports car introduced to the public at the U.S. Grand Prix in Watkins Glen, New York, in 1962. Unlike the Falcon-based four-seater that would reach production, the vehicle now known as Mustang I was a radical, mid-engined, V4-powered roadster with space-frame construction.

The four-cylinder engine was designed in Germany and made 109 horsepower at 6,400 rpm, not much by today's standards but quite a bit based on the car's extremely small body and light weight (1,148 pounds). Two radiators, one in each of the rear fenders, cooled the engine. It had a wishbone-front suspension with splayed coil springs and rack-and-pinion steering.

Mustang I's interior was equally unusual. The seats were not adjustable, but the pedals and steering wheel were. All instrumentation was placed directly in front of the driver, behind a proper three-spoke steering wheel.

Styling was anything but conventional. The Mustang I bore little resemblance to anything that preceded it and looked nothing like the production car that was soon to follow.

At Watkins Glen, the first Mustang scored a huge hit, which ironically persuaded Ford not to produce. Iacocca knew that those to whom the car appealed were too far outside the mainstream buying public for it to be successful.

Once the actual Mustang was given the green light for production, Ford unveiled the Mustang II show car, which bore a remarkable likeness to the soon-to-be-released automobile. It is impossible to look at Mustang II and not see the early '65 model. It had the C-scoop on the side, the running horse in an oval-shaped grille, and a three-bar taillight design. Unlike its predecessor, Mustang II had a conventional front engine, rear-drive layout, and an interior that screamed production-ready.

As experimental cars, both the Mustang I and II were wildly successful. They generated tons of press and created excitement wherever they went.

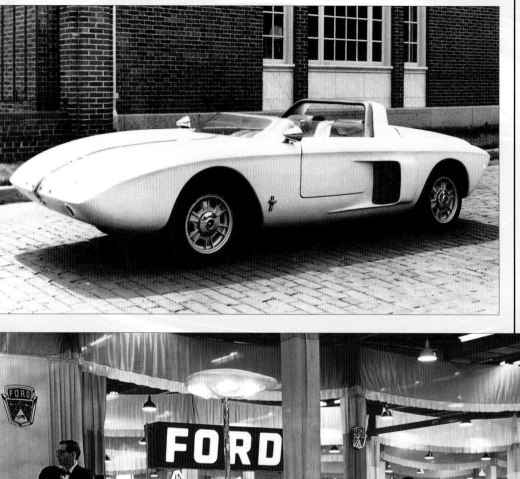

Mustang I (top) was a far cry from what eventually became the 1965 production car. It was a two-place, mid-engined roadster with a V4 for power. Its styling was radical, especially for 1962. Mustang II (bottom), on the other hand, was a thinly disguised example of what would soon be available in Ford dealerships across the country.

mission, and heavy-duty suspension. While this combo wouldn't let you run down guys in fuel-injected Corvettes, it was a spirited package that could more than hold its own at the Stoplight Grand Prix.

The number-one thing going for the Mustang, however, was that you didn't need the hottest engine to have fun. A standard convertible with a six-cylinder engine was a joy with the top down on a warm spring night. A 200-horsepower 289 coupe was the ideal car for driving to work or college in.

And thanks to the longest option list in the industry, you could tailor your Mustang specifically to be your Mustang.

On the downside, because the Mustang was based on the Falcon, its chassis was somewhat less than cutting-edge. There were no independent rear suspensions, à la Corvette or even Corvair. There were simple coil springs up front, longitudinal leaf springs in the rear, and a worm-and-ball steering box. Stepping up to the optional handling suspension gave you stiffer springs front and rear, bigger and better shocks, quicker steering, and a thicker front sway bar (0.84-inch versus 0.69-inch in the standard model). In a road test of a late '65 fastback in its October 1964 issue, *Car and Driver* magazine called the use of the Falcon rear suspension the car's most serious design flaw, stating that even with the heavier springs, it did not "provide notably better axle location."

Car and Driver did admit that the feel of Mustang's optional quick ratio steering was noticeably better than the standard: "it does handle—especially on smooth roads. The excessive understeer of the basic V8 model has been refined into a well-balanced characteristic that permits throttle steering (power-on understeer, power-off neutrality) on all turns up to 55–60 mph entry speeds....Driving the hot Mustang is a sensational—if noisy—experience."

AND THE BEAT GOES ON

Unquestionably, the Mustang set the automotive world on its ear. Production for the abbreviated early 1965 model year (March 1964–August 17, 1964) totaled 121,538. It absolutely crushed the Plymouth Barracuda, a Valiant takeoff with a fancy glass fastback (a paltry 23,443 sold),

which was actually introduced two weeks before the Mustang. Sales of the two-door versions of the Corvair Monza and turbocharged Monza Spyder totaled 126,429, but that was over the course of an entire model year.

The Mustang was not only on its way to dominating the marketplace, but it actually would create an entire niche of competitors, flatteringly called "ponycars."

For the beginning of the 1965 model year, Ford refined the Mustang, lengthened the option list even more, and added a fastback body style (known as the 2+2). It was the most exciting-looking of the three. If you ordered a fastback, the formal square roof and rear-quarter windows disappeared; in their place was a sleek, curved

The genealogy of the first-generation Mustang (from the bottom up): the Mustang I concept car, the Mustang II concept car (which bore many of the production car's styling cues), the 1965 coupe, and the 1965 Shelby GT350.

SUPER STANGS: SHELBY MUSTANGS 1965-1966

Carroll Shelby, a Texan who had enjoyed a great deal of success as a driver, had turned the road-racing world upside-down in 1962 with the Cobra, a hybrid sports car that put American V8 power in the tiny British AC roadster. It annihilated the Corvette, sending the beautiful new Sting Rays away in shame—something that pleased Shelby to no end since he had been rebuffed by Chevrolet when he had approached the company about putting its small-block V8 in the Cobra. Flush with the success of his all-conquering Shelby Cobra, Carroll Shelby turned his attention to Ford's ponycar.

When Ford came to Shelby about creating a series of high-performance Mustangs, it was a natural extension of their current relationship. Not only could Shelby make cars perform, but he was a larger-than-life figure, infinitely quotable and full of Texas charm. It didn't hurt that he was internationally famous, either. When he touched the Mustang, it was major news.

Remarkably, it didn't take much for him to transform the Mustang 2+2 from a fun, sometimes muscular, automobile, into a road-racing terror in the Sports Car Club of America's (SCCA) B-production class, giving another spanking to the Corvette.

Cars were delivered from Ford's San Jose plant to Shelby's facility in Los Angeles, where they went through the transformation process. All the Mustangs left San Jose as 271-horse 289 fastbacks; thus, minimal engine modifications were needed. An aluminum high-rise intake manifold with a 715-cfm Holley carb replaced the stock equipment, and a set of tubular Tri-Y headers carried away the exhaust through high-flow mufflers and pipes that exited on the side of the car, just aft of the doors. The cam was also changed, to a somewhat radical 306-degree duration, 0.457-inch lift grind. With these changes, the engines were now rated at 306 horsepower at 6,000 rpm.

The extra power made the stock brakes—marginal at best on a regular Mustang—completely inadequate. Shelby specified Kelsey-Hayes 11-inch ventilated discs up front, and sintered metallic linings for the 10-inch rear drums. A set of function scoops were added to the sides to cool the rear brakes.

For 1966, Carroll Shelby (right) improved visibility by adding rear quarter windows to the 2+2's roofline. This eliminated a bad blind spot. Functional air scoops for the rear brakes were mounted just ahead of the tires.

To improve cornering, the Shelby Mustangs—dubbed GT350s for no known reason—were lowered and fitted with Koni adjustable shocks. The inner pivot of the upper control arm was moved down an inch to increase negative camber. The stock 0.75-inch front sway bar was replaced with a 1-inch piece. A Monte Carlo bar and cowl brace added bracing to the underhood area, and the steering ratio was quickened for better response. A Detroit Locker differential helped put all the power to the pavement, and aluminum wheels with speed-rated Goodyear tires rounded out the package.

The interior came with a large tachometer and smaller oil-pressure gauge, but the backseat was removed entirely, replaced by Shelby with a fiberglass shelf. The spare tire was relocated on top of the shelf to improve weight distribution. Gone, too, was the standard steering wheel, replaced by a 16-inch wood-and-aluminum piece more conducive to high-performance driving. Three-inch-wide competition seat belts superseded the factory items. All cars were delivered without radios, though dealers could add them later.

Removing the rear seat saved a lot of weight, and the addition of a fiberglass hood made the car even lighter (about 120 pounds less than a stocker). A popular color motif for the Shelby Mustangs was white with Lemans blue stripes running the length of the body. Just less than 200 were shipped and dealers applied stripes to already white cars. Although not many were sold, the twenty-five R-model (race only) cars did very well in competition, taking the B-production title away from Corvette in 1966.

For '66, Ford civilized the GT350s a bit—but only a bit—to make them more appealing to a wider audience. The noisy Detroit Locker was gone, and the backseat returned. An automatic transmission was optional. Five new colors were added, including Guardsman Blue, black, and red. Even Hertz got into the act, ordering 1,000 Shelbys for its rental fleets—almost all of which received the automatic transmission. This helped push '66 Shelby production figures to 2,380.

It was the beginning of a Mustang partnership that would continue, with varying degrees of success, through the end of the decade.

Ford comes up with a real stopper!

Ford has a funny idea that when we give our customers big engines and high power-to-weight ratios for super go, we really ought to match it with super braking power to stop. That's why we've put front disc brakes as *standard equipment* on Mustang GTs, Ford 7-Litre models and Thunderbirds. (Power assist is part of the package on Fords and Thunderbirds.)

And we don't limit this kind of super stopping power to our hottest machinery either. We know that lots of people have special braking needs; like a station wagon hauling a trailer down steep grades, or a lot of brake-heating stop and go in someplace like San Francisco. That's why we've made front disc brakes available on any of the big Fords regardless of engine size and on *every* Mustang V-8.

Ford not only gives you discs . . . but puts radial ventilating ducts between the friction surfaces of the discs to pump air through the *inside* of the rotors. That's the coolest! Ventilated discs make Fords virtually immune to fade, you can stop again and again and again! So pick your favorite Ford, Mustang V-8 or Thunderbird and go, man, go . . . we can provide the stop!

YOU'RE AHEAD IN A FORD ALL THE WAY!

FORD

Above: Ford marketed the Mustang beautifully, making posters, models, and even children's pedal cars available to a public that seemingly couldn't get enough of Mustang mania. Following page: Styling changes were subtle for 1966. The rear quarter panel trim was revised, while the cross-hairs in the grille were deleted, thus giving the illusion that the galloping horse emblem was floating in the cavity. Three 289 V8s were available, with 200, 225, and 271 horsepower.

roofline that made the Mustang look like no other car on the road. It went a long way toward toughening the Stang's appearance. While convertibles and coupes could be described as cute, the 2+2 was mean-looking. Add the high-strung, high-po 289 for $327.92, and it was mean-acting as well, capable of low 15- and high 14-second quarter-mile times on the meager tires of the day. Certainly not an all-out drag-strip burner, but a satisfying car, thanks to its decent handling (a heavy-duty suspension was standard with the hi-po 289), light weight, and 6,000-rpm capabilities.

Car and Driver recorded rather remarkable acceleration figures for the K-engined Stang that it tested in its October 1964 issue. Equipped with the optional, and certainly drag race–oriented, 4.11:1 rear axle gears, the 2+2 accelerated from 0 to 60 mph in a blazing 5.2 seconds and covered the standing quarter-mile in 14.0 at 100 mph. These were extraordinary times for this car, and it is doubtful that many production cars could have duplicated them.

"We got acceleration figures almost in the Cobra class with the 4.11 ratio, but this made it an impossible car on the highway," noted *Car and Driver*.

While the drag-strip gears may have made for some noisy cruising, they helped the Mustang show its taillights to its two main competitors. Neither the Corvair nor the Barracuda could touch it. In a test of the top-of-the-line Formula S Barracuda in *C&D's* October 1964 issue, the best that Plymouth's entry could muster was 9.1, 0–60, and 17.5 at 88 mph in the quarter, though *C&D* did heap high praise on its handling.

MUSTANG MILLS

Like the rest of its components, the Mustang's engines were fairly straightforward, uncomplicated designs. The early '65s came standard with the 170-cubic-inch six-cylinder engine, which produced a reliable but uninteresting 101 horsepower. Smart shoppers stepped up for one of the available V8s. The 260 two-barrel, dubbed the "Challenger V8," put a few more strides in the Mustang's gallop, thanks to its 164 horsepower. The other early '65 engines were both 289s, the first a 210-horse four-barrel version, the second the high-performance 289 with 271 horsepower.

Available for just a few hundred dollars more than the six-cylinder, the 271-horse 289 came with such race-inspired features as 10.5:1 compression, slightly domed pistons, a high-lift, solid-lifter camshaft, and a special intake manifold with a larger Autolite four-barrel carb than the 210-horse 289.

Only the 271-horse 289 made it to the late '65 and '66 Mustangs. The standard six-cylinder engine became the 200-incher with 120 horsepower, while the 260 disappeared forever in favor of the 289, a crisp engine that seemed just about the perfect size for the first-generation Stangs. The two-barrel carbed version made a reasonable 200 horsepower, and the four-barrel/hydraulic-lifter cam 289 made 225.

While the high-performance 289 option made the Mustang a strong runner, thanks to its 271-horsepower, the Shelby GT350 upped the ante to 306, thanks to improvements like steel Tri-Y exhaust headers, an aluminum intake manifold, and Holley carb.

Among the more interesting options you could stuff into your Mustang was the GT Equipment Group, introduced in April 1965. The standard instrument panel had a flat, horizontal speedometer that was too reminiscent of Ford's lowly compact for the comfort of some. For only $165.03, an upgraded instrument cluster was available, with genuine gauges instead of warning lights. Each gauge came in its own round pod, and it helped to mask some of the car's Falcon roots. Another option was the Special Handling Package, which included quick ratio steering, rocker panel stripes, chrome exhaust tips, and grille-mounted fog lights, among other things. This became available after April 1965.

One month earlier, Ford released what is now known as the "Pony interior." Officially called the Interior Decor Group, it featured embossed horses galloping across the seats, plus the upgraded five-gauge instrument panel—all for $107.08. This would turn out to be money well spent because the Pony interior is one of the more sought-after options by collectors today.

A buyer could opt to remove the seat belts and receive a $10.76 credit (this was 1965, after all).

Despite its low base price, you could add enough extras to your Mustang to swell its price to well over $4,000—a handsome sum back then, enough to put you behind the wheel of a nicely equipped Corvette. This little car, the same vehicle that many feared would be the next Edsel—Henry Ford II had told Lee Iacocca that his job was on the line with this one— was making Ford an awful lot of money. There were 559,451 late '65 Mustangs produced, including more than 77,000 fastbacks and more than 110,000 convertibles. Ford's three plants (Dearborn, Michigan; San Jose, California; and Metuchen, New Jersey) were working at a fever pitch, but they weren't at full capacity yet. That would come in 1966.

It helped that the late '65 Mustang was a genuinely better car than it had been only months earlier. As mentioned previously, the standard six-cylinder engine was upgraded to 200 cubic inches. And while the 260 V8 was okay, the more potent 289s gave even the 200-horsepower Mustang a nimbleness that just couldn't be found in other small, compact cars.

With things going so well, it should surprise no one that Ford did little to upset Mustang sales for 1966. It revised the styling slightly, with changes to the grille, the

While the Mustang hardtop was rather formal looking, this view of the 2+2 fastback shows just how sleek a Mustang could be. This is a '66 GT.

hubcaps, the gas cap, and a few other areas. Backup lights and rear seat belts became standard features, and the louvers on the side of the fastback's roof remained functional. Amazingly, the list of optional equipment topped 100 items, including dealer-installed goodies. Mustang buyers could get things their way.

Factory engine choices were a carryover for '66, with the 120-horsepower 200 six standard and three versions of the 289 optional. Horsepower on the V8s remained the same—200, 225, and 271—yet fewer buyers opted for the top engine: sales of that motor fell from 7,273 to 5,469. That may be the only area where Mustang sales faltered, as the total number of cars produced increased to 607,568. Remarkably, Ford still had no real competition. The Corvair Monza and its top-of-the-line Corsa brother sold just 58,422 units, despite a striking redesign a year earlier. The Plymouth Barracuda, which got a new grille in '66, fared even worse, at 38,029.

While many people in the United States were caught up in Mustang mania in late 1964 and early 1965, Ford's engineers were already readying the car's first redesign. The Mustang was going to be on a two-year cycle, meaning that it would be revamped in '67, '69, and '71. Ford understood that it wouldn't have the market to itself forever (it was, in fact, introducing a competitor called the Cougar from its own Mercury division) and was well aware that Chevrolet had a ponycar all its own coming shortly. Further, it realized the soon-to-be-introduced Camaro would have honest, big-block engine muscle behind it. Knowing this, Ford began designing a larger, heavier car whose engine bay would accommodate a 390-cubic-inch or larger engine.

Before the last of the first-generation Mustangs rolled off the assembly line, Ford was already straying from Iacocca's original vision of a small, lightweight, sporty car and preparing to enter the muscle-car wars.

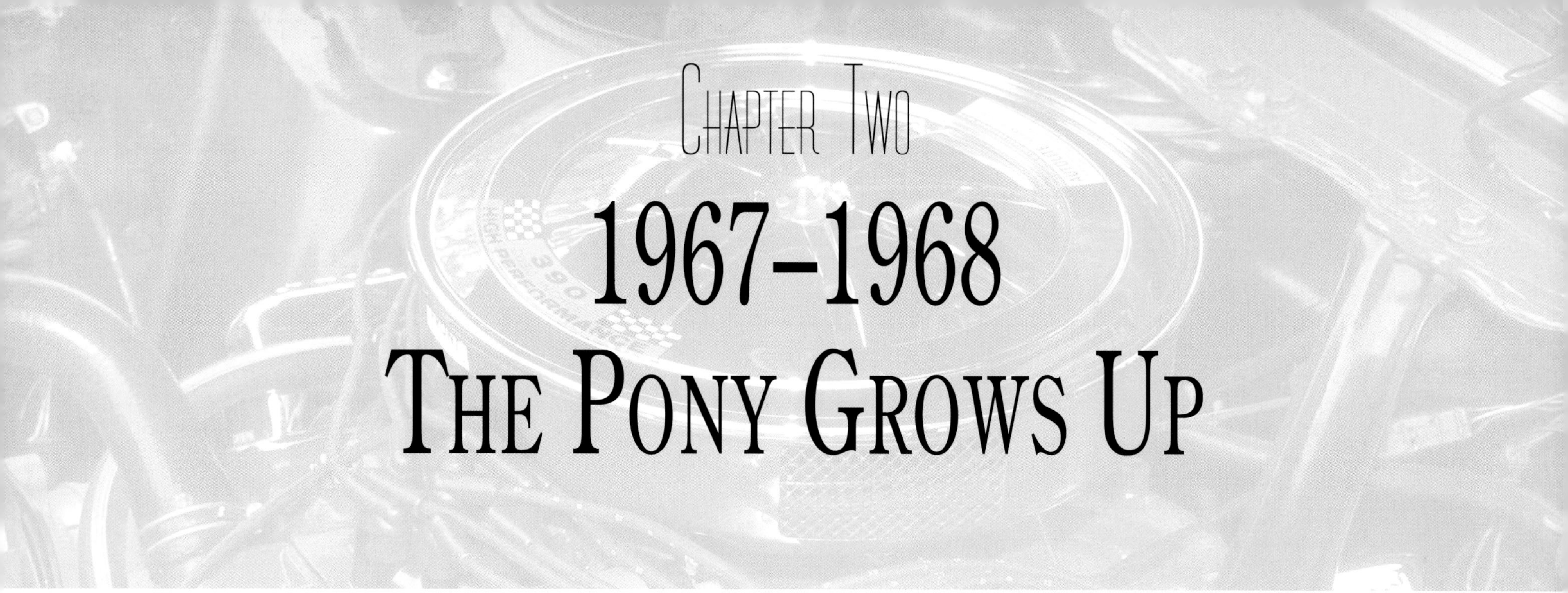

CHAPTER TWO

1967–1968
THE PONY GROWS UP

The Summer of Love. *Sgt. Pepper's Lonely Hearts Club Band*. The Monterey Pop Festival. Psychedelia. The year was 1967, one of the craziest, wildest times to be young in America. The country had changed, and so had the Mustang. With the introduction of the '67 models in September 1966 the Mustang became larger, heavier, and more powerful. Its chassis was improved, it was more comfortable, its handling became more athletic. And for the first time, it had some real competition in the marketplace. In 1967, Chevrolet, Pontiac, and Mercury would introduce worthy adversaries; in 1968, even tiny American Motors would join the fray.

For two and a half years, Ford's Mustang rang up billions of dollars in revenue for the Blue Oval. But rival manufacturers did not just sit on the sidelines. Chevrolet secretly readied the Camaro, all the while claiming that the Corvair was a better, more sophisticated car than the Mustang. Plymouth, which actually beat the Mustang to the market by a couple of weeks with the Barracuda, was working feverishly on a complete makeover for that unpopular fish, one that preferably wouldn't leave such an odor in the showrooms.

Pontiac had enjoyed great success since the fall of 1963 with the GTO, an intermediate stuffed full of big-inch, multi-carbureted muscle. The man behind that image

The Mustang grew larger in 1967 and the popularity of big cubic-inch muscle cars influenced the entire line. The engine bay was widened to accomodate the large 390 engine from Ford's passenger cars and a new Shelby, the GT500 (pictured here), came standard with a special 355-horse, 428 cid V8.

machine was a legend in the car business—John Z. DeLorean, a rebel at conservative General Motors. As the head of Pontiac (the "Excitement" division of General Motors), he resisted the urgings of others who wanted a ponycar. For years, DeLorean had had a different idea. He had been pushing for an inexpensive two-seater based on the Banshee show car, a sort of poor man's Corvette, rather than a Mustang fighter. Economics, however, dictated that there was more money to be made with a four-seater than with a pure sports car, and so eventually it was decided for him that Pontiac would indeed have its own version of the four-seat Camaro, and to hell with his cheap sports car. Thus, the Firebird was born, albeit a few months after the Chevy.

Mercury dealers, feeling left out (especially since the Mustang was creating stampedes in Ford showrooms), were blessed with a ferocious kitty named the Cougar. In actuality, it was just a gussied-up version of the Stang, but it was marketed as a low-buck Jaguar. Thanks to a richer interior and dynamic styling, it worked the same magic for Mercury that the Mustang had for Ford; it was the best-selling new car in the division's history.

All the ponycars were very successful, especially the Camaro, which benefited greatly from Chevrolet's popularity among young people and its performance image. But the competitors did little to check the flow

of customers (or enthusiasm) for the original. In what was something of a down year for the auto industry, Mustang sales remained robust.

BIGGER, BETTER, FASTER

As was customary in the world of automobiles, major redesign work began on the Mustang before the jury was in with a verdict on its first incarnation. A team of product planners, stylists, and engineers had already started plotting the changes by the summer of 1964. It may seem odd, but this was the norm for the auto industry until the late seventies and early eighties, when a crushing onslaught of government regulations made bi-annual redesigns grossly inefficient and costly. In the old days, car design was, in many ways, as much a crapshoot or guessing game as fashion design. More than today, the way a car looked went a long way toward determining how it was received in the marketplace.

From the very beginning, those who designed the Mustang were well aware of many of its engineering shortcomings, and looked forward to remedying them. The truth was that any car built on a budget off of Falcon underpinnings could probably use a bit of help.

And the Mustang got help. Ford's goals included improving the ride and handling, providing a more comfortable and accommodating interior, and enlarging the car enough so that it could accept the 390-cubic-inch big-block V8. At this point, the muscle-car era was in full swing, and as sweet as the hi-po 289 was, it was starting to wilt from the heat in the street-racing wars. Also, Ford soon realized that if Chevrolet was to answer the Mustang challenge, it would surely employ the powerhouse 396, its latest big-bore V8, an engine that in very little time had already garnered quite a reputation on road and track—especially in 425-horse Corvette trim.

While the '67 Mustang was essentially a complete revamping, the wheelbase remained unchanged at 108 inches. However, the front suspension was redesigned and the track (front and rear) widened by 2 inches. Not only did this improve ride and handling, but it enabled the engineers to shoehorn the 390 FE-mill.

At the same time, overall width increased by 2.7 inches, the car sat a half inch higher at the roofline, and

The runaway success of the Mustang spawned a host of imitators, aptly nicknamed "ponycars." Among them were the Pontiac Firebird (top), which shared its platform with the Chevrolet Camaro, and the Mercury Cougar (bottom). The Mustang and Cougar shared many of the same parts, as well as the chassis, but the Mercury was more upscale, more luxurious, and naturally, more expensive.

overall length increased by 2 inches. Thanks to its new styling, however, the '67 Mustang appeared much bigger than it actually was. The grille opening, while maintaining many of the original car's styling themes, was massive where it had once been trim. The taillights, now housed in a concave panel, were also larger, though they retained the three-bar design—soon to be a Mustang trademark. The C-shaped indentation of the sides remained, but the side scoops just ahead of the rear tires were restyled. If your '67 Mustang had the Exterior Decor Group, it received a hood with two indents housing engine-compartment scoops and turn signal indicators visible from the driver's seat.

Three body styles continued to be offered: hardtop, convertible (now with a two-piece glass rear window available), and a "faster" fastback. While the roofline on the '65–'66 2+2 ended just ahead of the trunk, now the Mustang had a true fastback, one that sloped to the end of the deck lid.

Was it a successful restyling? Certainly, the new Mustang was a handsome car, especially the fastback, but much of the simplicity of the original was gone. From certain angles, it appeared bulkier and ungainly. From others, though, it was definitely more intimidating.

"This [redesign] makes the new Mustang look like it's ready to pounce at you from the front, or high-tailing it away from you from the rear," said the December 1966 issue of *Motor Trend*, in a story that introduced the new model to its readers.

The editors at *Car Life* liked it, too: "The overall styling is a sleek, harmonious improvement over the 1966 Mustang....Despite dimensional alterations and subtle changes in shape, the overall appearance of the fastback is still totally Mustang."

Inside, a thorough revamping stripped away whatever was left of its Falcon roots. While the dual-cockpit design carried over, the instrument panel was all new. Two large, round gauges—one on either side of the steering column—dominated, with three smaller round instruments supplying the ancillary information. If the buyer ordered air conditioning, it was now integrated into the dash panel, rather than being an auxiliary "knee-knocker" hanging below the dash.

For an extra $108.06 (less for convertibles), the prospective Mustang buyer could order the Interior

The Mustang could be all things to all people. If you desired an all-out drag car, you ordered the fire-breathing Shelby GT500 (top). Something hot but less outrageous? The coupe with the GT package (center) would fit the bill nicely. Of course, for open-air cruising, few cars could match the convertible (bottom). Enough options were available to make it quite luxurious, extras like power windows, air conditioning, and "Stereosonic" 8-track tape player.

Right: Styling on the '67 Mustangs
was evolutionary. The grille cavity
was enlarged, the roofline was more
dramatic, and fake air scoops
appeared in front of the rear tires.
Also, the taillights were now concave. Fog lights, as seen here, were
part of the GT Equipment Group package. Bottom, right: The V8 engines
were carried over from 1966, with
the exception of the heavy, powerful
390 FE big-block, which produced
320 horsepower.

Decor Group, which provided aluminum inserts in the
instrument panel and on the doors, but no longer
included the galloping pony insets in the seats.

Other interesting interior options were a redesigned
console, which ran the length of the floor and then up the
front to be integrated with the radio (which could now be
ordered with an 8-track tape player), and the Tilt-Away
steering column, which not only allowed the steering
wheel to be adjusted, but actually swung away to the right
when the driver shut the key, placed the transmission in
"Park," and opened the door on that side. This allowed
much easier entry and exit, a big plus because without it,
the steering wheel ran very close to the seats and often
rubbed people the wrong way—especially those thick in
the thigh department.

Handling on the '67 Mustangs was greatly improved,
as was ride quality. Whereas the '65–'66 models had front
springs mounted over the upper A-arms, dimensional
changes allowed a lower roll center, and upgraded bushings were used, thereby decreasing understeer. This was
especially important with the heavy 390 engine, which

also required a much larger front sway bar. New rubber
bushings were used at suspension attachment points,
which helped to isolate road noise and shock, increasing
passenger comfort.

If you ordered the GT with either the high-performance 289 or the 390, the Competition Handling suspension—with even stiffer springs and shocks, a larger sway
bar, and 15-inch wheels—was available.

SNAKES ALIVE! SHELBY MUSTANGS FOR 1967-1968

With the market for more powerful muscle cars with enormous engines rocketing ever higher, it came as no surprise that Carroll Shelby started work on a big-block Shelby Mustang for 1967. But while Ford temporarily held the reins on the regular Mustang by keeping displacement down to 390 cubic inches, Shelby let the horse run wild. Shelby Mustang buyers in 1967 had two choices: the GT350, again with a 306-horsepower 289, or the new GT500, with a specially prepared 428 that cranked out 355 horsepower at 5,400 rpm and 420 foot-pounds of torque at 3,200. In addition, Ford offered two four-barrel carburetors on the GT500.

The 428 in Shelby's new model was an impressive piece. A pair of 600-cfm Holley four-barrels sat atop an aluminum medium-riser intake manifold. A special hydraulic lifter cam opened and closed the valves, and a dual point distributor helped provide the spark. Compression was a reasonable 10.5:1.

There was more to the new Shelby Mustangs than just horsepower. More interior amenities were available than in the '65–'66 versions. Both the GT350 and 500 had taken a step away from the racetrack and toward a grand touring machine. Shelby's engineers tweaked the suspension, which had already been revamped on the regular Mustang, to make it more compliant and less punishing than it had been. This was achieved in large part by using softer, adjustable Gabriel shocks (rather than expensive Konis), and stiffer springs.

To distinguish the GT350 and GT500 from their plebeian roots, Shelby called upon designers Chuck McHose and Pete Stacey to add some visual excitement to the cars. And did they ever! The nose was extended 3 inches, and the headlight buckets were altered as well. The grille-mounted headlights could be either center mounted or outboard (still inside the grille surround) depending on state law where the car was to be delivered. With their new twin-scooped fiberglass hood, the Shelbys looked more aggressive than any previous Mustang. But the designers didn't stop there. The rear deck received a spoiler and fiberglass tail panel with dechromed Cougar taillights. Side scoops similar to those on the '65–'66 GT350s were standard, too. The overall effect was startling. While some '67–'68

Shelby Mustangs now came in two flavors, the GT350 with the high-output, 306-horse 289 and the GT500, (below), which sported a 355-horse 428 topped with a pair of 600 cfm Holley four-barrel carbs. Once the 335-horse 428 Cobra Jet appeared in 1968, it replaced the Shelby 428 and came in a model called the GT500KR (for King of the Road).

Mustangs look a bit overweight, the GT350s and 500s were pure muscle.

While regular 390 Mustangs had trouble against their foes, the 428 Shelbys could run tire-to-tire with the best ponies from GM and Chrysler. They were capable of mid- to high 13-second quarter-mile times. Little could outrun them on street or strip.

Again, there were major changes in store for the Shelby Mustangs in 1968. The cars received another face-lift, with a revamped hood and nose. The air scoops were moved to the leading edge of the hood, and rectangular fog lights replaced the round driving lamps of the '67 models. Out back, '65 Thunderbird taillights replaced the Cougar units from the year before.

Under the hood, the big news was the introduction of the 390 "Thunderbird Special" V8 engine. A member of the FE (Ford Engine) family, the 390 first appeared in 1961. It was a bored-and-stroked version of the 352-cubic-inch big-block introduced in 1958. With a 10.5:1 compression ratio and a 600-cfm Holley four-barrel carburetor, the 390 made 335 horsepower in the Mustang and 427 foot-pounds of torque, quite an improvement on paper over the old Hi-Po 289. Given the fact that the 390 cost substantially less than its smaller, less powerful cousin, it should come as no surprise that the 390 dealt a crippling blow to sales of the K motor. Just 472 High-Performance 289s were sold, compared with 28,800 390 GT and GTA (for "automatic transmission") models. After 1967, the K-code 289 would disappear forever.

But was the 390 Mustang that much faster? Not really, especially in stock trim. *Motor Trend*, *Hot Rod*, and *Car Life* each tested '67 390 Mustangs, and the quickest of the bunch was *Hot Rod's*, which turned a 15.31 at 93.45 mph in the quarter-mile, though this automatic-equipped version benefited from loosened accessory drive belts, an old speed trick designed to free up a couple of extra horsepower, and tweaked throttle linkage. *Motor Trend's* totally stock four-speed GT went 15.6 at 94 mph, while *Car Life* registered a 15.5 at 91.4 (with two people aboard).

As we noted in the first chapter, '65–'66 hi-po 289s could run these numbers or better. In defense of the '67

cars mentioned here, however, they were all fully laden with weight-adding and power-robbing accessories, like air conditioning, Tilt-Away wheel, and tape decks. Also, the 390 Mustangs had 3.00:1 or 3.25:1 highway-style gear ratios, rather than the 3.89 and 4.11s drag race–oriented gears of the early cars.

The year 1967 was also when Plymouth dropped its 383 in the Barracuda, Chevy its 396/375-horse bomb in the Camaro, and Pontiac its 400 in the Firebird. How did the Mustang stack up against this trio? Unfortunately for Ford lovers, not very well. While the Mustang and big-block Plymouth were a fairly even match, both of GM's offerings were significantly quicker in a straight line. Even Chevy's 350 small-block Camaro was a half-second and 2 mph quicker in the quarter, according to *Hot Rod*.

Opposite: Ford cleaned up the styling of the Mustang for '68. Gone were the rear quarter panel scoops. C-stripe, road wheels, and tailpipe tips were all part of the GT package. Concave taillights were introduced a year earlier and were gone by 1969. Left, top: When fitted with the 428 Cobra Jet, the Mustang took a backseat to no one when it came to performance. A functional cold-air hood scoop was available to duct cold, dense air to the carburetor, thus increasing performance. Left, bottom: The ponycar's interior grew more comfortable, more upmarket with each passing model year. Consoles, wood trim, and air conditioning (now integrated into the dash) became increasingly popular. Following page: As with the first generation Mustangs, the fastback 2+2 was preferred by the high-performance crowd. Now a true fastback, the roofline again deleted the roll down windows for rear seat passengers.

MUSTANG GT/CS AND HIGH COUNTRY SPECIALS

If there is any doubt that southern California was the center of the hot car universe in the sixties, think about this: about 20 percent of all Mustang sales were in the greater Los Angeles area. This did not go unnoticed by Lee Grey, the Los Angeles Sales District Manager, who was looking for a way to bolster sales in 1968 amid increasing competition.

At the time, Shelby American was toying with the idea of producing a notchback version of its GT350 and GT500. One prototype, nicknamed Little Red, had been built, and Grey took notice of it. Fitted with a Shelby hood, taillights, side scoops, and so on, it was ready for action. Grey got hold of Little Red and showed it to dealers, customers, and his staff. Although Shelby decided against adding the car to its model lineup, the reaction Grey received was favorable enough that he pitched the idea of a Los Angeles–area Mustang to Lee Iacocca himself. After making its way through

miles of red tape, the idea was approved by Ford Motor Company, and the Mustang GT/California Special was born, although the plan was expanded to include eleven different sales regions in western United States and Canada, not just L.A.; Ford decided to let northern California dealers also receive the GT/CS.

Fourteen separate items made up the GT/CS package, including a Shelby-like fiberglass rear deck lid and end caps, fiberglass rear panel housing '65 Thunderbird taillights, nonfunctional Shelby side scoops, unique California Special and GT/CS lettering and striping, and hood pins. The galloping Mustang emblem that usually floated in the grille was removed, and two rectangular fog lights filled in at either end. The grille itself was painted a metallic dark gray.

About 4,325 GT/CS Mustangs were produced, according to the *GT/California Special Recognition Guide* by Paul M. Newitt. Of these, 300 were built as High-Country Specials, a near-identical model that was sold in the Denver area. Every Mustang engine from the 200-cubic-inch six to the 428 Cobra Jet was available. Because of their rarity and similarity to the Shelbys, the GT/CS and High Country Specials are prized today by Mustang lovers.

A direct follow-up to the '68 GT/California Special was the High Country Special (opposite and above), a near-identical model sold in the Denver area. Both cars were inspired by a prototype Shelby coupe that never reached production.

Still, Ford enjoyed the last laugh. Even though sales of the Mustang in 1967 were down significantly from the banner year before (472,121 sold vs. 607,568), Ford destroyed the challengers in that particular race. Camaro was the sales runner-up with 220,906 sold, followed by Mustang's sister car, the Cougar (150,893), and the Firebird (82,560), which wasn't introduced until the middle of the model year. Plymouth moved only 62,534 Barracudas.

Fortunately for Ford mavens, all-out domination in the performance wars was but a few short months away. The savior would be called Cobra Jet.

As was the case two years earlier, the Mustang received only a mild face-lift for '68. All three body styles returned, but the fake air vents ahead of the rear tires were remodeled into a single vertical bar that was integrated into the body's side C-scoop. The horizontal bars in the grille disappeared, never to return. Government-mandated side markers appeared on the front and rear quarter-panels and all '68 Mustangs came with chrome rocker moldings.

Inside, the three-spoke steering wheel was replaced by one with a single, fat center section that ran its width. For the first time, Mustang bucket seats were equipped with seat-back locks to keep them from folding forward during quick deceleration or panic stops.

Thus did the Mustang continue down its middle-of-the-road path, providing fun and excitement for the masses. But what was there for those who demanded more, the lunatic fringe of the automotive world? This was the pinnacle of the muscle-car era, after all. While the 390 was certainly a large enough engine for a smallish car like the Mustang, it simply wasn't getting the job done from a high-performance perspective. The 390 had rarely been pushed for any kind of work other than propelling Thunderbirds and Galaxies, its three-deuce variants of 1961 being the exception. By the late sixties, it had a reputation on the street for being a stone. Something had to be done, and Ford knew it.

On April 1, 1968, Ford answered the prayers of the Blue Oval faithful everywhere when it unleashed the 428 Cobra Jet to the general public. Ford wisely introduced this model at the National Hot Rod Association's Winternationals in Pomona, California, two months earlier. Underrated by the factory at 335 horsepower, the Cobra Jet Mustangs dominated their classes, serving notice that the company from Dearborn wasn't willing to roll over and play dead for the competition.

The 428 Cobra Jet had good, big-valve (2.097-inch intake, 1.66 exhaust) heads, similar to those on low-riser 427s, but with bigger ports. It had a 10.7:1 compression ratio and breathed through a cast-iron version of the 428 Police Interceptor intake manifold topped by a 735-cfm Holley four-barrel carb and functional ram air hood. The cam was the same hydraulic-lifter piece that came in a 390 GT, but the exhaust manifolds were redesigned for freer flow. For durability, it had beefier connecting rods, larger rod bolts, a nodular iron block and crankshaft, and a high-pressure oil pump.

Even on the limiting street tires of the day, it was capable of mid-13-second quarter-mile times, equal to or better than anything the competition had to offer.

"We knew it didn't have the race potential of, say, a 426 Hemi, but on the street it was damn near unbeatable," said Bill Barr, a Ford engine engineer who worked on the Cobra Jet project. "We had a red notchback version at our Arizona test track and—I'll never forget this car—it ran a 13.4 at 104 mph, box-stock at high altitude."

All Cobra Jets came with staggered rear shocks to eliminate wheel hop and power front-disc brakes for an added measure of safety. You had your choice of transmissions with the 428: a C-6 automatic or a Top Loader four-speed. If you ordered your CJ Mustang with 3.91 or lower gears, you got what was known as a Super Cobra Jet, which benefited from an engine-oil cooler and 427 cap-screw connecting rods.

As *Hot Rod* was quick to point out in its March 1968 road test, the competition—accustomed to nothing but 289s and 390s—didn't know what hit it. "All the frustration was put out of mind the first time we let it happen—waaah—the secondaries open and you realized most races would end right there, in low gear. The would-be competitor can't believe his eyes. No Mustang outside of Tasca's 'Mystery 7' has moved this quickly before....Such is Ford's great leap forward—the Cobra Jet. The mere fact these Dearborn rocket sleds are coming off the production line deserves some kind of award or other."

Finally, Ford had a ponycar that could take home the trophies at the drag strip, as well as on a road course. This model is highly prized among collectors and is still a

Big-block power arrived in non-Shelby Mustangs in the form of the 390 in 1967. For 1968, the 390 was detuned slightly and the 428 Cobra Jet became the top engine.

very competetive vehicle in stock and superstock drag-racing. Nonetheless, the increased competition in the marketplace was diminishing the Mustang's market share. Total sales for the Mustang slipped for the second straight year, to 317,404, a trend that would not reverse itself until 1973. Mercury's Cougar sales stumbled as well, down to only 113,726. The competition was beginning to carve out a serious piece of the ponycar pie. Forever-financially-strapped American Motors even made money in the ponycar market. It introduced two new models, the AMX, which had only two seats, and the Javelin, which was essentially a stretched AMX with a backseat. By selling 56,462 Javelins and 6,725 AMXs, American Motors managed to turn a profit for the first time in many years.

Ford planners must have thought the best defense against all this was a good offense, because in 1969 it offered the craziest horse yet.

The 428 Cobra Jet engine debuted at the 1968 Winternationals (below) in Pomona, California, and was an instant success, winning its class. It hit the streets somewhat later, in April, both in the Regular Mustang and the Shelby GT500KR (opposite).

CHAPTER THREE

1969–1970
A THOROUGHBRED AT LAST

Every field has its greats—those who define it for all who follow. In the world of sports, for example, it is the talented few who become legends. Babe Ruth forever changed the game of baseball with his mighty home-run swing. On one fateful evening, Wilt Chamberlain scored 100 points in a single game of basketball. Secretariat, perhaps the greatest racehorse ever, shattered racing records everywhere en route to capturing the Triple Crown, and he captivated an entire nation with his heroic exploits.

True greatness doesn't come often, not in the world of sports and certainly not in the world of automobiles, where it can be swept away with one swipe of an accountant's pencil.

After four model years of blistering sales and unparalleled public acclaim, the Mustang became a true thoroughbred in 1969. Its styling was the best yet—longer, lower, and wider, in the time-honored American tradition—and its performance capabilities were unequaled. Four new models debuted, one more exciting than the next, along with four new engine options. The interior evoked images of expensive Italian sports cars, but without masking its American muscle-car heritage. Even the Shelbys were completely redesigned, so much so that they were barely recognizable as Mustangs.

Styled steel wheels were a $116.59 option on most '69 Mustangs. They were standard on the Mach 1, but not available on the Grande or 200-inch 6-cylinder versions.

There was a lot of Shelby influence in the design of the 1969 Mustang, especially the fastback version, which was now dubbed the "SportsRoof." It bore a striking resemblance to the '67 Shelbys, with a larger, more aggressive grille cavity with four headlights, a sleeker fastback with a built-in ducktail spoiler, swoopy lines, plus scoops on the hood and sides. It was an intimidating car. The only question was, would it be too intimidating for the traditional Mustang customer?

VARIATIONS

Of the five new models that were widely available in 1969, one was a luxury coupe, three were straight-ahead performers, and one was a rare economy model with a 200 c.i.d. automatic six and ultra high rear axle for maximum gas mileage. The Grande, available as a coupe only, was as upscale as the Mustang got in the sixties. Like its Mercury cousin, the Cougar, it sported wood-grain appliqués on the instrument panel and console. There were also thicker carpeting, plusher seat covers, and 35 pounds of extra sound-deadening material.

To improve its ride—an area in definite need of assistance—Ford used softer springs and shocks, plus different bushings in the rear springs. *Car Life* called the '69

Grande "brisk, nimble, quiet and stable." It was also pleas-
antly surprised by its handling: "The Grande's cornering
power was higher than a luxury ponycar is expected to
have."

The first of the three new performance models introduced was the Mach 1. Built only as a SportsRoof, it took
full advantage of every sexy line that the body offered.
The hood was painted flat black and came with a nonfunctional hood scoop and hood pins. Reflective stripes ran
down the middle of either side and across the back panel.
Dual racing mirrors were part of the package, as were the
Deluxe Decor Group for the interior and the Competition
Suspension. All Mach 1s got the Grande's extra sound
insulation, a handicap at the drags, but a blessing if you
ordered one of the hairy optional power plants. The standard engine was one of the new ones, the 351 two-barrel
V8, which made 250 horsepower. Priced to move, the
Mach 1 cost just $504 more than a base SportsRoof
model.

Engine options consisted of a 290-horse, four-barrel
version of the 351, the 390, which was down to 320 horsepower, and the Cobra Jet and Super Cobra Jet versions of
the 428. Either could be had with Ram-Air induction. It
consisted of a scoop mounted directly to the air cleaner
that stuck up through a hole in the hood. Many opted for
"the Shaker" hood scoop; so-called because of its ten-
dency to rock with the engine.

The motoring press went wild for the Mach 1. *Car Life*
called it the fastest four-passenger vehicle it had ever
tested, and asked, "Are you ready for the first great
Mustang?" With two men aboard, a full tank of fuel, and
no tuning tricks to the Cobra Jet engine, it ran a best of
13.86 at 103 mph, which prompted this comment: "The
Mach 1, then, goes like the hammers in a straight line."

What amazed the *Car Life* test drivers was that a
Mustang with such a large engine could handle as well as
it did. "By choosing the optimum combination of suspension geometry shock-absorber valving and spring rate,
Ford engineers have exempted the Mach 1 from the laws
of momentum and inertia, up to unthinkable speeds."

Part of its exceptional handling came from the optional
Goodyear F70-14 Polyglas rubber, not so wonderful by
today's standards, but cutting-edge street-tire technology
for the sixties. They were part of the Mach 1 package
with the 428; 351s and 390s got regular-issue E70-14s.

Said *Motor Trend*: "You will want [the 428CJ] not so
much because it turns the Mach 1 into one of the fastest
cars in the world, but that the Ford suspension men have
done such a lovely job of distributing the great weight of
the engine....They created a machine that handles like a
Trans-Am sedan."

The Mach 1 created a sensation in showrooms as well.
An astounding 72,458 persons put one in their garage that
year—nearly 25 percent of all Mustang sales for 1969. It
was such a smash that the GT package, still available on
the hardtop, convertible, and SportsRoof, became superfluous. Only 5,396 ordered the GT option, and it disappeared at the end of the model year.

The other two new models were actually specials,
brought to market to showcase two exceptional new
engines. These were the Boss Mustangs, built around
race-bred power plants that needed production homes to
make them eligible for competition.

The more nimble of the pair was the Boss 302. Ford
had actively participated in the Sports Car Club of
America's Trans-Am series since its inception, winning the
championship in 1966 and 1967. But a tough season followed, as Chevrolet's Camaro Z/28 simply dominated in
1968 and 1969 as well. It didn't help matters that Ford had
been without a super-strong small-block since it did away
with the high-performance 289 after the 1967 model year.
Engineer Bill Barr took the canted-valve heads from the

soon-to-be-released 351-Cleveland engine and mated them to the 302. The result was a high-winding mill that was lightweight, reliable, and powerful—a flawless combination for road racing and the perfect antidote for the Bowtie problem. (The Camaro Z/28 was beating the heck out of Ford in Trans-Am racing.) It also filled a void in Ford's product line.

Street-going versions of the Boss 302 got a special graphics treatment designed by Larry Shinoda, the main pen behind the '63 Corvette Sting Ray, the highly acclaimed '65 Corvair, and the '68 Corvette, an automobile that created a sensation at the time and lived in slightly modified form until 1982. Shinoda was lured away from General Motors when Semon E. "Bunkie" Knudsen left Chevrolet to become president of the Ford Motor Company in 1968. Knudsen was a giant in the industry, who almost singlehandedly re-created the Pontiac Division in the fifties. Under his guidance, it catapulted from sixth in sales to third, behind Chevrolet and Ford. He took over as the number-two man in the company behind Henry Ford II when the Deuce snubbed general manager Lee Iacocca because of a clash of egos.

Shinoda kept the basic goodness of the Mach 1 and further refined it. He kept the flat-black hood, but removed the scoops and the fake air intakes on the rear fenders. The flat-black paint treatment continued on the taillight panel and deck lid, to which a matching, adjustable wing was added. The headlight buckets were also blacked out, and a backward C-stripe with the Boss 302 logo adorned the sides. A front spoiler helped keep the nose down at speed, while rear-window louvers kept the sun from baking passengers through the giant fastback glass. "Boss" was Shinoda's nickname for Knudsen; it was also part of the era's slang—if something was very hip, it was really boss.

What made the Boss sing? The engine itself was beefed up for racing with four-bolt main bearing caps, forged-steel connecting rods, and a stronger forged-steel crankshaft. A 10.5:1 compression ratio made premium fuel mandatory. A 300-degree duration mechanical cam opened the monstrous 2.23-inch intake and 1.71-inch exhaust valves, which were really too much for a street car. In fact, Ford even specified smaller valves in 1970. A large 780-cfm Holley four-barrel atop an aluminum highrise intake fed the fuel, which, once burned, was carried away by 2.5-inch exhaust pipes.

Left: Ford engineers reduced the size of the intake valves on the 1970 Boss 302 engine, the result of which was a more responsive street engine.

Below: The Mustang did away with quad headlights in 1970 after only one year. In an unusual move, they kept the inboard mounted lights, eliminated the outboard lights, and replaced them with fake air intakes.

While it was a little short of power at low rpm, it could pull all the way to its factory-installed rev limiter at 6,000 rpm. It made 290 horsepower at 5,800 rpm and 290 foot-pounds of torque at 4,300, and was capable of propelling a Boss 302 to high 14-second quarter-mile times. Not bad, but the car's true forte was its handling.

Standard on the Boss were wide 7-inch chrome and argent-painted five-spoke Magnum 500 rims with F70-15 Polyglas rubber, quick-ratio power steering, and stiffer springs and shocks.

It was an impressive package, but not capable of holding off the Camaros on the track—yet. The Roger Penske Z/28, driven by the late Mark Donohue, had one of the greatest racing seasons of any type in 1969 to capture the Trans-Am championship. The Boss 302's greatest moment came when it won the 1970 T-A crown.

MEET THE BIG BOSS

In 1963, Ford had embarked on what it called its "Total Performance" campaign. It was out to dominate every form of motor sports on the planet and was willing to

The hardtop body style was ideal for racing since it was the lightest. This is a rare Super Cobra Jet version, which (for just $6.53) gave the engine stronger connecting rods, crankshaft, and flywheel, plus added an engine oil cooler when you ordered either 3.91 or 4.30 gears.

spend millions of dollars to win races. One of the most important venues was NASCAR stock-car racing, in which—since the introduction of the Chrysler Hemi-head engine—the Ford team had not fared as well as it had wanted to. Ford had been using its Torino and Mercury Cyclone intermediate-sized muscle cars in NASCAR races and had even built an aerodynamic droop-snooted version of both cars in an attempt to be more competitive, but the Chrysler Hemi dominated. In an attempt to catch up to Chrysler, the Blue Oval engineers designed a modern hemispherical-head engine of their own, the Boss 429.

When it came time to homologate the new Boss 429 engine, Ford went through a ridiculous amount of trouble to put it into the Mustang. To fit the Boss 429, with its massive, extra-wide cylinder heads, into the Mustang, the engineers had to redesign the front suspension completely and widen the engine compartment. The front suspension originated as standard on the 428 Cobra Jet, but the upper A-arms were moved out a half inch and lowered an inch. The lower arms were moved outboard to increase camber, and the front spring rate was stiffened. Actual production of the car was too intensive for

Larry Shinoda: Eighteen Months of Fame at Ford

Livonia, Michigan, is a long way from Manzanar, the infamous Japanese internment camp in California's Owens Valley during World War II. Today, Livonia is home to Shinoda Design Associates, which can draft anything from a body kit for a late-model Mustang to a motor home. Its founder is Lawrence K. Shinoda, the legendary stylist whose credits include the 1963 Corvette Sting Ray and '69–'70 Boss Mustangs.

Shinoda, born in Los Angeles to Japanese-born parents, was forced with his family to go to Manzanar when he was a twelve-year-old student at Burbank Junior High. He survived that experience and grew up to be a typically car-crazed southern California teenager. After graduating from the Art Center College of Design in Los Angeles and the Douglas Aircraft Technical School, he landed a job with the doomed Studebaker-Packard company, where he worked for only seven months before securing a position at General Motors in September 1956. By 1959, he was working on Bill Mitchell's Sting Ray Sports Racer project, the body of which would become the inspiration for the production '63 Corvette.

He stayed with Chevrolet until May 1968, when he followed Bunkie Knudsen to Ford. He was put in charge of all high-performance production cars, show vehicles, displays, and exhibits, but like Knudsen, he was viewed as an outsider, an interloper from arch-enemy General Motors.

"There was a lot of resistance against my working at Ford, mainly from [then vice-president of design] Gene Bordinat," Shinoda said. "I ended up starting at two pay grades lower than I was supposed to. It was a real uphill fight."

Although he only stayed at Ford for eighteen months before getting canned—first Henry the Deuce unexpectedly fired Knudsen; without his benefactor, the designer's days were numbered—Shinoda was one of the busiest people in Dearborn. The Boss 302 was his first project, and later came the Boss 429, the Torino Talladega and Cyclone Spoiler I and II, and the ill-fated King Cobra.

Most recently, Shinoda is responsible for the Rick Mears Special Edition Corvette and the Boss Shinoda stripe-and-body kit for '94–present Mustangs. In the interim, he designed motor homes, revolutionized the trucking industry with his streamlined White tractor (which, thanks to its slippery shape, helped improve fuel economy by 25 percent), and designed race team uniforms, among hundreds of other things. He continues to speak his mind about what he considers good and bad when it comes to automobiles.

For many, the 1970 Boss 429 Mustang is the ultimate of the breed. Its race-inspired engine, unique styling, power, and performance make it among the most highly sought-after collector's cars of the muscle car era.

a fast-moving assembly line, and had to be farmed out to Kar Kraft of Brighton, Michigan.

In street trim, the engine itself is a bit of an oddity. Despite the incredible flow capabilities of the semi-hemi heads, Ford saw fit to outfit the Boss 429 with a mild hydraulic cam and a 735-cfm Holley carb—a fuel mixer smaller than the one used on the little Boss 302. Fortunately, Ford didn't scrimp on the good stuff when it was time to assemble these engines. All received four-bolt mains, forged-steel cranks, and connecting rods. The heads were aluminum and of the dry-deck variety, meaning that they didn't use head gaskets to seal them to the block. Instead, each cylinder, oil, and water passage had its own O-ring to seal it. Pretty radical for a street car, but horsepower checked in at "just" 375, not even close to its potential. In stock trim, it was about an even performer with a ram-air Cobra Jet.

Graphically, the Boss 429 differed substantially from the Boss 302. There was no flat-black anything, nor were there window slats or a rear spoiler. This car was all business. An oversized hood scoop ducted cold air to the carb, a front spoiler kept it planted at speed, and the Boss 429 nomenclature was stenciled in outline letters on either front fender.

While the Boss 429 dominated the NASCAR circuit in the midsize Torino body, the competition put up a strong fight in the salesroom. Mustang production dipped from 317,404 in 1968 to 299,824 in 1969. In hindsight, some have blamed the Mustang's increased size and weight for hurting sales, and though this may have had something to do with it, the fact is that all cars were increasing in size as the sixties wound down. People liked bigger cars and bought them by the million. But the Camaro kept improving, in design, power, and overall comfort, as did the Firebird, Barracuda, Javelin, and Cougar. As their names implied, it was a jungle out there.

Actually, 1969 was a bad year for ponycars. Only Camaro sales, bolstered by an extra few months of production, climbed, from 235,147 to 243,085. The Firebird slipped from 107,112 in 1968 to 87,709; the Cougar went from 113,726 to 100,069; Javelin sales fell by over 20 percent, from 55,124 to 40,675; and Plymouth's Barracuda, never a hot commodity, plummeted from 45,412 to 31,987, despite the introduction of a 440-cubic-inch V8 engine, the largest ever offered in a ponycar to that point.

SHELBY MUSTANGS—THE END OF THE LINE

In 1995, when Ford first approached Carroll Shelby about building hot street and race Mustangs, the company wanted top-of-the-line ponycars. The market, however, changed rapidly. The Shelby Mustangs went from being barely civilized race cars for the street to softer, plusher, grand touring cars almost overnight. Once Ford took over production in 1968, it became a Shelby in name only. That year, options like air conditioning and automatic transmission became available, as did a convertible model. They were great cars, but not the enormous step up that they had once been.

Ford introduced the Cobra Jet to its entire line in 1968. The GT500 was available with the C.J. and was called the GT500KR or "King of the Road" model. Meanwhile the GT350 became a shell of its former self. Gone was the stinging 306-horse 289; in its place was a passenger car–like 302, making only 250 horsepower. The only way to squeeze any performance out of a '68 GT350 from the factory was to order the optional Paxton supercharger, which increased horsepower to 335 at 5,200 rpm and torque from 318 foot-pounds to 325. Still, this was expensive, and few people bothered. They really wanted the big-block, anyway.

By 1969, the transformation to a high-performance, grand touring car was complete. The new Shelby Mustangs had the same suspensions offered in the Mach 1 and, except for the 390, the same engines.

What made the '69 Shelbys desirable then (and now) was the styling, which was totally different from that of the standard Mustang. The only body parts shared by the two were the doors, roof, and rear quarters. More than twenty fiberglass parts were used, including the front fenders and hood (which saved 70 pounds—a big plus for performance). The grille area offered a preview of what the '71–'73 Mustangs would look like, and the fiberglass hood had a total of five NACA ducts; some drew cold air into the carburetor; others extracted hot air from under the hood.

Fastbacks and convertibles differed slightly. The nonfunctional side scoops on the former were situated where the fake scoops on the Mach 1 were, while those on the convertible could be found in their customary place, just ahead of the rear wheels. The taillight treat-

Above: The 1969 Shelby Mustangs bore little resemblance to their Mustang brethren. The unique styling was due, in large part, to a fiberglass front end that had an oval-shaped grille and five hood scoops (three for ducting cool air to the engine and two that removed hot air from the engine compartment). Convertibles, introduced to the Shelby lineup in 1968, all received rollbars.

ment was similar to that of the '68 Shelbys, but now there were rectangular dual exhaust tips that exited together beneath the license plate.

Wheels and tires were unique to the Shelbys, too. Fifteen-inch, five-spoke mags carried F60-15 Goodyear tires.

So un-Shelbyish were the new versions, with their emphasis on luxury and cruising, rather than racing, that *Car and Driver* called its GT350 "a garter snake in Cobra trim." Only 3,150 Shelbys were sold in 1969, and just 601 '70s left the lot. In actuality, the '70s were leftover '69s that were given updated serial-number plates, different hood stripes, and front spoilers. When they slipped away, almost no one noticed, nor did anyone care.

Below: While the GT500 still moved quite well thanks to the 428 Cobra Jet, the enthusiast press was none too kind to the GT350, which sported a 290-horse 351. *Car and Driver* called it a "garter snake in Cobra trim," while *Super Stock & Drag Illustrated* wrote, "the 350 version of the 1969 Shelby GT is a lot of beautiful car going places slowly."

THE STAMPEDE IS OVER

By now, Ford had so many horses in the corral—Mach 1s, Bosses, Grandes, Shelbys—that it was getting difficult to keep them straight. Ford thinned out the herd a bit by discontinuing the GT for 1970. The lumbering 390 was also history. Still, there were nine possible engines available in ten different models.

As was the norm, refinements were made in the even-numbered year of the two-year cycle. Larry Shinoda left his mark on the third-generation Mustang by cleaning it up a bit. In an unconventional move, he reduced the number of headlights from four to two by discarding the outboard headlights. The inboard headlights remained in the grille cavity, and simulated scoops replaced the outboard lights.

The side scoops were filled in à la 1969 Boss 302, and the taillights were now recessed in the rear panel. The design was cleaner, smarter, and less aggressive, although the Boss 302's rear wing and window slats became available on all SportsRoof models.

A triple-stripe treatment (one wide stripe with thinner outboard ones) running the length of the hood replaced the flat-black hood treatment on the Mach 1. The Boss 302's got a similar stripe, but had other stripes that ran down the sides of the fenders and toward the rear of the car.

The newest engine was a 351, called the Cleveland (for the city where it was built). Its most important feature was its canted-valve cylinder heads, which had debuted on the Boss 302 a year earlier and made it a natural-born heavy breather. Ford and Mustang lovers didn't know it then, but the 351-C would become a staple of Blue Oval performance for years to come.

To improve street performance, smaller intake valves were used in the Boss 302, from 2.23 inches to 2.19. They improved both throttle response and mid-range torque.

The much-heralded Boss 429 was actually the most understated performance Mustang; the only thing that gave it away was the giant gloss-black scoop on the body-colored hood and the understated Boss 429 nomenclature on the fenders.

There wasn't a lot not to like about the '70s Mustangs, as the refinement and performance were as good as ever. But it was getting harder than ever to insure the high-

performance muscle cars—the rates were too high, and some companies wouldn't insure them at all. Neither the Boss 302 nor 429 would return for 1971. They had done their jobs, and Ford was getting out of the racing business. Perhaps the youth market had simply had enough of these beasts; even with gas at just 30 cents a gallon, these thumpers could send you to the poor house fast. Even a small engine like the Boss 302 got just 10–13 miles per gallon. A 428 CJ with the Drag Pack might be lucky to get 6 mpg. They could also be temperamental and finicky, requiring constant tuning. Who needed the hassles?

Government edicts concerning engine emissions were starting to take effect as well. Soon all the major manufacturers would be lowering compression ratios, leaning out carburetors, and designing vehicles to run on unleaded fuel. Once the OPEC oil embargo came in the early seventies, the muscle cars—not to mention the muscle Mustangs—would go away, if only temporarily.

But before this would happen, performance would have one last stand.

Left: Interest was waning in the Shelby Mustangs by 1969 and few magazines were able to test them. *Super Stock & Drag Illustrated* **did get its hands on a 4-speed GT500 in its September '69 issue and ran a very respectable 13.87 at 104.52 in the quarter-mile. Above, right: When equipped with the optional 300-horse 351 Cleveland engine ($48 extra), the Mach 1 Mustang became an inexpensive, strong running junior supercar. Right: Playboy Pink was not a regular production paint code for the Mustang in 1969, but in the less-than-politically-correct sixties, it failed to offend.**

CHAPTER FOUR

1971–1973
THE END OF THE LINE

With the introduction of the 1971 redesign it finally happened. Ford completely and forever abandoned the original concept of the Mustang—small, nimble, inexpensive. At this time, Ford was building some of the largest land yachts ever, and plans were in place for them to keep growing. Ford expected its full-size cars to weigh over 5,000 pounds in the near future—enough to classify them as trucks. When the company's engineers were drawing the blueprints for their 429 engine, they designed in the capability to enlarge it to well over 500 cubic inches.

Certainly, you couldn't blame them for trying: the American public showed little resistance to these barges. They were status symbols. Even if you couldn't afford a Lincoln Continental, there were other, less expensive, cars that were almost as big. Real men drove real cars; small cars were for hippies and women.

At least that was the thinking in Detroit. So, yes, the '71 Mustang was the largest ever, but in actuality, it wasn't quite as big as it looked. The car's styling, which echoed Ford's late sixties mid-engine LeMans racing efforts, made it appear enormous. However, the '71 Mustang was but a scant 1.5 inches longer than its main competitor, the Chevy Camaro, and over 2 inches shorter than the Pontiac Firebird and Dodge Challenger.

Ford stylists were on a two-year cycle, so it was no surprise when the 1971 Mustang appeared with totally revamped sheetmetal. The front end was reminiscent of the '69–'70 Shelby Mustangs and the entire car was larger. A new model, the Boss 351 (pictured), replaced the Boss 302 and its performance was equal to or better than the 429 Cobra Jet now available in the Mustang. Still, only 1,806 Boss 351s were eventually sold.

The car—it seems too large to call it a ponycar—was virtually all new. Its wheelbase was stretched to 109 inches, the front track widened 3 inches to 61.5, the rear 2.5 to 61. Weight was also up, especially with the new big-block 429 Cobra Jet.

Except for the front end, which resembled the '69–'70 Shelbys, and the three-bar vertical taillight motif, the '71 Mustang bore almost no likeness to any of its forerunners. Its near-horizontal SportsRoof, which earned the nickname "flatback" from some, and "aircraft carrier" from Larry Shinoda, was definitely bold, as was its steeply raked (for the time) windshield. The Mustang was lower than before, and the side windows were narrow; combined with the blind spots in the rear quarters that were created on both the coupe and the fastback, seeing out was definitely an adventure.

"It's like sitting in a bunker," is how *Car and Driver* described it. "You can hardly see out. The windows are gun slits."

The magazine did admit, however, that it was an attractive car. "We aren't condemning its appearance. In fact, that side of it is generally attractive—striking, rather than beautiful, but it turns more than its share of heads."

Said *Sports Car Graphic*: "The new body gives one the feeling of being buried in a bunker....We have returned to the bulbosity of the '49 Merc."

The Boss 351 had the highest base price of any Mustang in 1971 ($4,124), but came standard with serious high performance hardware like a 3.91 Traction-Lok differential, four-speed manual transmission, competition suspension, and a Ram Air hood. Under the hood, the 351 Cleveland-based mill featured a solid-lifter camshaft, 11.0:1 compression ratio, a four-bolt main block, and special cylinder heads with larger ports—good enough to make 330 horsepower.

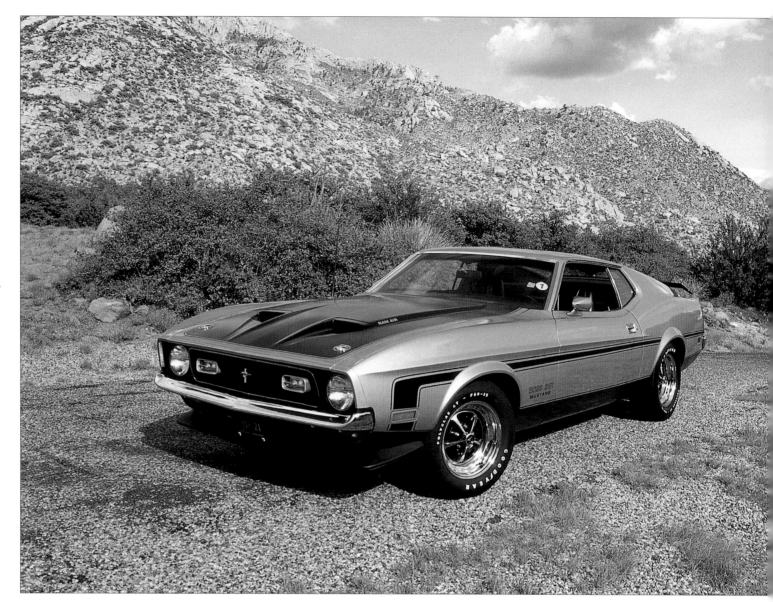

Which was probably the point. Young people generally like to sit low behind the wheel, thinking that if they can't see out, well, then probably no one (including the police) can see in, either. Mach 1s got a honeycomb grille with "sport lamps," tuned competition suspension, and new striping. They also got color-keyed front bumpers.

Ford certainly wasn't bashful in its advertising. "'71 Mustang. New style and handling from the Trans-Am winner," the copy read. "Mustang has always meant outstanding roadability and nimble handling.... And 1971 brings you even more Mustang. Wider tread. Lower stance."

There was a lot of model reshuffling in the Mustang lineup. The Mach 1 remained, though the standard engine was now the 302 two-barrel. The 428 Cobra Jets bit the dust, replaced by the 429 Cobra Jet and Super

Cobra Jet, which were introduced the year before in the Torino and Mercury Cyclone, but shared few parts with the now departed Boss 429. Confused? If you're not, you probably should be, but that's how Ford did business back then.

Gone also was the Boss 302, replaced by an even better engine, the Boss 351. This was a superhot (330-horsepower) version of the 351-Cleveland engine that came with a mechanical lifter cam, 750-cfm Autolite carb, 11.0:1 compression, and a host of bulletproof parts in the valve train and bottom end. Even though the 429s had an extra 78 cubic inches, they were no match for the Boss 351. Only 454 Corvettes and 440-six-pack Mopars were faster in 1971.

Car and Driver had no complaints about the performance of its '71 Boss. "It would repeatedly inhale its way through the quarter mile in 14.1 seconds at 100.6 mph." Power shifting dropped ETs to 13.9 at 102.

Mustang Prices: Cheap Thrills

Although the price of a new car today seems to jump by about $1,000 a year, inflation was not much of a factor in the sixties. In April 1964, the base price of a six-cylinder Mustang coupe was $2,320.96. By 1973, the price of that same combo had risen only $440, to $2,760. A '73 convertible, at $3,102, was a mere $545 more than it had been in 1964.

What makes those figures seem even more remarkable is that the later Mustangs were better equipped, had more safety features, and were larger than their predecessors.

Mustangs received a mild facelift in 1973. The parking lights were now mounted vertically in the grille, rather than horizontally. Also, the bumper was larger, redesigned to meet new federal crash standards. This would be the last year for a Mustang convertible until 1973. Despite its increased size and weight, the Mach 1 Mustang was still a hot performer when properly optioned. This one has the 370-horsepower 429 Cobra Jet engine, previously only available in Ford and Mercury's midsized muscle cars. Color-keyed bumpers and dual racing mirrors were standard on the Mach 1 in 1971.

ROUND AND ROUND THEY GO:
THE MUSTANG IN TRANS-AM COMPETITION, 1966–1972

For the first six years of its existence, the Mustang benefited tremendously from Ford's participation in racing, particularly the SCCA's Trans-Am series. Suspension engineers picked up invaluable knowledge in the road-racing arena and applied it to special models like the Boss 302 and Boss 351.

It was partly because of the Mustang's early success that the Trans-Am series was born. The SCCA created the series so that European cars and these new American "sedans"—the Mustang, the Barracuda, the Dodge Dart, and the rear-engined Chevrolet Corvair—could battle it out across the country. Two classes were formed, the under-2.0-liter division for the Euro cars, and the over-2.0-liter for the Americans.

The first race was run in 1966 at the 12 Hours of Sebring in Florida. Of the forty-four starters in the Trans-Am, only nine were over-2.0-liter cars, including three Stangs, three Cudas, two Corvairs, and a Dart. The Dodge, driven by Bob Tullius, finished second overall, the best showing for the domestic iron.

The Mustang was victorious at the second Trans-Am race, and won again in the fourth outing (in which Mustangs finished in first and second place). Going into the last race of the year, at Riverside, California, the Mustangs and the Darts were tied with thirty-seven points apiece. Eight Mustangs entered, three of which were racing under the Shelby backing, which meant factory support—vehicles, money, parts, and R&D. Jerry Titus won the race in a Mustang, followed by Tullius's Dart, giving Ford the championship.

(It is interesting to note that all the Mustangs entered in the series were coupes. The fastback Shelbys had already made a name for themselves in B-production; this was an opportunity for the plainer coupes to get some exposure and accolades. The factory cars wouldn't be fastbacks until 1969.)

As the ponycar wars heated up, so did the Trans-Am. It expanded to twelve races in 1967, and Ford fielded several teams, with the Mustangs under the supervision of Shelby and a three-Mercury team spearheaded by Bud Moore. Moore actually assembled a veritable motor-sports all-star team. His drivers consisted of road-racing legends Dan Gurney and Parnelli Jones, NASCAR heroes Cale Yarborough and LeeRoy Yarbrough, and Peter Revson and Ed Leslie. Shelby enlisted the services of Titus and Dr. Dick Thompson, the "Flying Dentist," who was famous for winning SCCA titles in the Sting Ray Sports Race Car earlier in the decade.

Chrysler had pulled its support, but Chevrolet got more heavily involved, especially with the Camaro of Roger Penske and Mark Donohue. As expected, 1967 was a battle royal, but not between the Fords and Chevys. Instead, the Mustangs and Cougars scratched and clawed at each other. Against all odds (the Mercury teams always got less factory support than the Fords), the Cougars actually led the Mustangs by one point going into the season finale in Kent, Washington. Donohue's Camaro won the race, but the Mustang of Ronnie Bucknum finished second, ahead of Gurney's Cougar, to give the championship to the Mustangs.

Maybe what Ford saw scared some folks, but from that point on, it fielded only Mustangs in Trans-Am competition. Although Jones and George Follmer drove the cars, it was tough racing for the next two years. The Penske/Donohue/Camaro combination was nearly unbeatable, winning ten of thirteen races in 1968. Camaros won eight times in twelve tries in 1969, with Donohue in the winner's circle for six of them.

They were lean years for Ford, but the Mustangs fared much better in 1970. It didn't hurt that Penske and Donohue switched to AMC, where they spent a season sorting out a new combination. But no one just handed the crown to the Boss 302. It was a damn fine race car, and Moore's team of Follmer and Jones captured the T-A title with a combined six victories.

Unfortunately, 1970 was the last year for some time that Ford actively participated in racing. For 1971, it was up to the independent teams to carry the Blue Oval into battle. And they didn't do too badly. While Donohue led AMC's Javelin to the championship (and earned the first-ever

Ford had cut its racing budget by 75 percent in 1970, but there was still enough green for Bud Moore to campaign a pair of Boss 302s in the Trans-Am series (driven by Parnelli Jones and George Folmer). Ford won the manufacturer's title that year for the first time since 1967.

Trans-Am driver's championship, with eight victories), Ford scored twice with Follmer behind the wheel of Moore's Mustang (he also finished second five times).

By 1972, only American Motors still fielded a factory team. Ford was out of racing, trying to get ready for an onslaught of emissions regulations and preparing a new, smaller Mustang.

Though still sporty, the Mustang's interior was moving more toward comfort and convenience by '73. The steering wheel, for instance, could be found in a host of other Ford sedans.

In deference to the car's newfound extra weight, the previously optional 250 c.i.d. six-cylinder engine was now standard. All 351 V8s were now of the Cleveland variety, making 240 (two-barrel), 285 (four-barrel), or 280 (Cobra Jet—very rare) horsepower.

Moving up to the big-blocks were the 429 Cobra Jet and Super Cobra Jet. All C.J.s had 11.3:1 compression, four-bolt mains, forged rods and pistons, and canted valve-style heads. Regular Cobra Jets had hydraulic lifter cams and Rochester Quadrajet carburetors and were rated at 370 horsepower.

Buyers opting for the Drag Pack (3.91, 4.11, or 4.30 gears) got the Super Cobra Jet engine instead. A 780-cfm Holley carb replaced the Quadrajet, and an oil cooler was added, as was a mechanical lifter cam with an adjustable valve train. For some reason, it too was rated at 370 hp, though if you ordered Ram Air, 375 ponies were on tap.

While a Ram Air 429 SCJ is a rare animal, with only 610 Drag Pack Stangs built in 1971, this writer had the opportunity to write a shoot-out article some years back, featuring one such beast. It ran consistently low 14-second times: 14.34, 14.42, and 14.29, all in the neighborhood of 98–99 mph, which is representative of what these cars ran when new.

Changes to the interior were many. The speedometer and optional tach were still directly in front of the driver, but the ancillary gauges were relegated to the center of the dash near the floor, out of the driver's line of sight. The steering wheel, straight out of Ford's family sedans, was also new, and completely out of synch with the rest of the car's sporty nature.

Though its radical shape and larger dimensions may have alienated some buyers, it was still the best-selling car in its class, by some 35,000 copies over the Camaro.

Perhaps the worst part of 1971 was that it was the last year that Ford fans could get a big-block ponycar. By 1972, the largest engine available was a 351. Two years later, you couldn't even buy a V8—any V8. Only a four-cylinder and V6 engine were offered.

Even Ford must have felt that the party was over. Compression ratios dropped across the board in anticipation of low-octane unleaded fuel. Virtually no changes were made from a styling standpoint in 1972 or 1973, though the parking lights in the '73s went from horizontal to vertical. Sales were so bad for the Camaro and Firebird in 1972 that there were rumors that the cars would be canceled. Only the Pontiac would continue to offer a big-inch engine through the seventies, the 455.

Unofficially, the high-performance Mustang era came to a temporary close in 1972. The stalwart efforts were the 351 H.O., which was basically a low-compression version of the Boss 351 that made 275 horsepower. Fewer than 1,000 were built, and all came with 3.91 gears, four-speed transmissions, dual exhausts, and competition suspensions, among other goodies. There was also the 351 Cobra Jet (266 hp), another variation of the Cleveland mill.

One special model, the Sprint, was introduced. It sported a patriotic red, white, and blue paint scheme, with white being the main color.

By 1973, the decision was made to downsize the Mustang, for car-buyers who preferred smaller, sportier cars to the land barges. Hence, the '73 models were the last of the original breed. For the first time since 1966, sales of the Mustang increased, especially the convertible, which, it was announced, was going out of production. Regular Mustang sales jumped from 125,093 to 134,867, with convertible sales nearly doubling, from 6,401 to 11,853. Mach 1 sales also remained strong, with more than 99,000 being sold from 1971 to 1973.

Ford Motor Company, and especially Lee Iacocca, now the president of the company, thought it was time to return the Mustang to its roots. The year 1974 would see the introduction of the Mustang II, a vehicle that succeeded wildly in spite of itself.

Optional since 1969 was the rim-blow steering wheel. Just squeeze the steering wheel rim (above, top) and the horn blows—no fussy buttons to push. After 1971, the largest engine available in the Mustang was a 351 (above, bottom). By 1974, no V8s would be offered, a dubious first for the original ponycar. It would be 22 years—1995—before a 351 would again be offered in the Mustang. The last of the first-generation Stangs were the 1973s (right). Following page: Despite its increased size and weight, the Mach 1 Mustang was still a hot performer when properly optioned. This one has the 370-horsepower 429 Cobra Jet engine, previously only available in Ford and Mercury's midsized muscle cars. Color-keyed bumpers and dual racing mirrors were standard on the Mach 1 in 1971.

Chapter Five

1974–1978
Score: Mustang II, Performance 0

For some people, the 1970s meant the resignation of President Richard M. Nixon. For others, the end to the war in Vietnam was the main event of the decade. Musically, the breakup of Crosby, Stills, Nash & Young, the mega-success of the Bee Gees, and the disco craze all came to symbolize this period. There was the Iran hostage crisis and runaway, double-digit inflation.

For America's gear-heads, however, the most important single event of the seventies was the Arab oil embargo of 1973. When OPEC turned off the juice and the nation's supply of gasoline trickled to a halt, the door was all but slammed shut on performance. Soon, lines at gas stations replaced those at the staging lanes of the local drag strip. If you could find fuel, chances were that you could only buy a limited quantity and you would be paying nearly double for the privilege. Suddenly, all the muscle cars, luxo-barges, and land yachts of the United States were up for sale at bargain-basement prices. Nine times out of ten, the owners couldn't give them away. The public went on a buying frenzy for anything small. Import dealerships couldn't keep their econoboxes in the showrooms. Big was out, and small was in.

And Ford found itself with another runaway success.

Back in 1971, when the newest Mustang was hitting the showrooms, plans were already underway for its suc-

Thanks in part to the first Arab oil embargo of 1973, the downsized, thrifty Mustang II became a runaway sales success for Ford when introduced in the fall of that year as a '74 model. The Ghia model (pictured) replaced the Grande as the luxury Stang. Ford borrowed liberally from the styling of the 1965 Mustangs; the size was also fairly close.

cessor. Lee Iacocca and the other executives in Dearborn had rejected the concept for an even larger Mustang car. They were responding, they said, to an ever more vocal group of customers who had complained about what had happened to its ponycar. The car had gotten too large, too garish, too inefficient. It had strayed from its roots as a small, exciting, economical sporty car. The next-generation Mustang, Ford decided, would return to its roots, become more slender, more practical, more fun.

There was a lot of evidence, even in 1971 and 1972, that this was what buyers wanted. Toyota's first-generation Celica was a hit, and the new Datsun 240Z was flying out of showrooms. Mercury had a certifiable smash on its hands with the Capri. Imported from Ford of Germany, it was billed as "the Sexy European," and was chock-full of the things that made the original Mustang so sought after. It was stylish and nimble, sipped fuel, and had sprightly, if not blistering, performance. Inside, it had many thoughtful touches, including full instrumentation, sculpted bucket seats, map lights, and other sporty accoutrements. Best of all, it didn't cost an arm and a leg to drive, maintain, or insure. Sound familiar?

Another important consideration was the public's acceptance of the Ford Maverick, an economical compact born in 1970. Available as either a two-door or four-door, the Maverick was an overwhelming sales triumph, with

450,000 finding homes in the first year alone. It further convinced Iacocca & Co. of the potential for a fun, sporty compact. Iacocca instructed Ghia, the Italian design firm that Ford had purchased in November 1970, to come up with a series of renderings for such a vehicle.

Armed with this knowledge, the plans for a larger Mustang were scuttled, and work began on a more

Ford's compact Maverick (left) proved overwhelmingly successful with consumers seeking reliable, inexpensive transportation. Viewed from the side, mid-sixties' Mustang styling themes—the formal roofline of the coupe and the C-shaped indentation on the side—were quite evident in the 1974 Mustang II (below). Price for the base hardtop crept to over $3,000 for the first time ($3,134).

diminutive automobile. To keep costs down, it would be based on the just-released Pinto platform. Power would come from either the Pinto's 2.3L overhead-cam (OHC) four-cylinder or the 2.8L V6 from the German-born Capri. Ford and Mercury designers then began working on the final styling.

The final product, introduced to a waiting world in the fall of 1973, was called the Mustang II. It borrowed a host of styling cues from the '65 Mustang—no surprise, since Ford was trying to catch lightning in a bottle for the second time in ten years. Placed side by side, the '65 and the '74 could easily be mistaken for father and son.

Two body styles were available: a coupe with a formal, squared-off roofline reminiscent of earlier models, and a hatchback that ended up looking more like the Pinto than Ford may have intended. Gone was the convertible— no surprise, since that body style had been on the decline in American cars for the better part of ten years. It had fallen victim to a rising crime rate in urban areas— your stereo and belongings were just the slash of a

switchblade away—and the increased popularity of air conditioning in new cars. Except for Jeep, other domestic manufacturers would stop producing convertibles after 1976.

Other styling touches that were lifted from first-generation Stangs were the long hood, short deck design, the C-shaped indentation on the side, the three-bar taillights, and single headlights flanking an oval grille.

Three models were offered: the base coupe, or 2+2; the Ghia, which filled the upscale slot formerly occupied by the Grande; and the "performance-oriented" Mach 1. We use quotation marks here because while the Mach 1 had a slightly revised suspension, it provided little in the way of acceleration.

Dimensionally, the Mustang II was quite a bit smaller and lighter than the '71–'73 models, and it was even more compact than the '65. Its wheelbase shrank from 109 inches in '73 to 96.2. Length decreased from 189.5 inches to 175—6.6 inches shorter than the early '65. It was also 4 inches narrower and a few hundred pounds lighter, though more portly than the '65.

While the minuscule backseat was carried over from previous Mustangs, the interior revealed radical changes. Gone were the sporty instrument panels and twin cockpit dash layouts. The Mustang II's office was a scaled-down version of Ford's flagship, the Thunderbird. It did have a rather complete gauge cluster, with full instrumentation. And taking a cue from some of Ford's best performers, like the Boss 429 and 428 Cobra Jets, the tachometer mysteriously lacked a redline.

As could be imagined, the suspension was completely revamped. Responsive rack-and-pinion steering replaced the old-style recirculating ball of previous Mustangs. The front springs moved from above the A-arms to between the control arms, front disc brakes became standard equipment. To control noise and vibration, an isolated front subframe was used with six rubber mountings. A front stabilizer bar was also standard to control body lean.

The rear suspension was a Hotchkiss-type with long 50-inch leaf springs. Staggered shocks were standard, meaning that the right one was mounted ahead of the axle and the left behind it, to control wheel hop, and improve traction during acceleration and braking.

These changes, combined with the sharp decrease in weight, improved the Mustang's handling substantially. Where the '74 Mustang II came up short was perfor-

Buoyed by the success of the Mustang II, Cobra II, Ford revived the '66 Shelby GT350H paint scheme of black with gold stripes. This is a '77.

mance. The base four-cylinder engine produced an underwhelming 88 horsepower, while the optional V6 provided only 17 more. That no V8 engine was offered was a real sign of the times.

If this lack of performance bothered anyone, it didn't seem to matter. Mustang sales almost tripled, going from 134,867 to 385,993. There was great joy in Dearborn, but it was short-lived. Despite the addition in 1975 of an optional 302 V8 (albeit an emasculated version, with just 140 horsepower), sales tumbled by almost 200,000 units. Part of the reason for this decrease in sales was that performance was starting to make a slight comeback. With the oil crisis easing up a bit, people could purchase as much fuel as they wanted, and didn't care that it was more expensive. But the engines were rough and unreliable, and the car itself could not hide its Pinto roots. Camaro sales, which had fallen off in the earlier part of the decade, had climbed back to around 150,000. Sales of a previously obscure Firebird model, the Trans-Am, began rocketing skyward. It bucked all trends, with its gas-guzzling 400- and 455-cubic-inch V8s. And while the insurance and safety lobbies had made performance a four-letter word, the Trans-Am boldly shouted it with a giant screaming-chicken hood decal and enough air dams, spoilers, and scoops to attract police from miles around.

Sales of personal luxury coupes also rebounded, and young people were more apt to choose a Mercury Cougar, Chevy Monte Carlo, or Pontiac Grand Prix than an undernourished pony like the Mustang II.

In an attempt to create some excitement in 1976, Ford introduced two new models, the Mustang II Cobra II and the Stallion. Both had garish paint schemes, the former recalling the glory of the original GT350, while the latter shared both the name and the color pattern with the Maverick and Pinto.

The Stallion was little more than a flat-black-painted Mustang II with silver sides and a couple of decals. It was pretty well ignored, both by the press and the general public.

Not so the Cobra II. By emulating the original GT350, Ford touched a nerve. It could be had in either white with blue stripes, or blue with white stripes (though Ford soon revived the Hertz GT350's black-with-gold color scheme). This turned out to be a good news/bad news situation. While buyers started snapping up Cobra IIs, comparisons with the original were inevitable, and there was no way the Cobra II could come off as anything but an impostor.

While the original Shelby GT350 was designed to be a barely streetable race car, the Cobra II was a cushy pretender, all fangs and no venom. The standard engine was, to the horror of many, the weak four-banger, and even the heavy-duty suspension was an extra-cost option. Both the V6 and V8 were available, but the 302 was choked by a two-barrel carburetor and single exhaust. At first, a four-speed transmission wasn't available with the V8, though it became an option later in the year.

Still, Ford's timing couldn't be improved upon. The Trans-Am (and the lesser Formula Firebird) had created a small uproar for performance cars, rekindling the hopes of those forced to go cold turkey by the combined forces of the insurance industry, the emissions gods, and OPEC. The Cobra II sold well at first, quadrupling first-year sales projections of 5,000. Even poster queen Farrah Fawcett drove one on the hit television series *Charlie's Angels*. (Partner Jacqueline Smith drove a Mustang II Ghia.)

But soon the word was out: the Cobra II was all false eyelashes and foam rubber. Performance was anemic— even four-speed 302 versions couldn't break out of the 17-second quarter-mile zone. While the T/A was no longer the straight-line missile that it had been in the late sixties and early seventies, it would absolutely destroy the V8

The Cobra II got a new treatment for 1978. The tape stripes that echoed the '65–'66 Shelby GT350 were replaced by this motif. It was not for the faint of heart or the bashful.

King Cobra: The Flashiest Snake Yet

Purists cringed when they first laid eyes on the King Cobra. How could Ford attach such a sacred name to such a cartoonish car? Well, this was the late 1970s, the heyday of flashy dressing, disco dancing, and Donna Summer. The King Cobra carried the Ford banner into the performance market with all the subtlety of a Fourth of July fireworks display.

The King Cobra option was the most expensive on a Mustang ($1,277) since the fabled Boss 429. It carried the 302 engine as standard equipment, as well as the heavy-duty suspension package.

Of course, the King Cobra's appearance was what made it special. Up front was an enormous air dam; just ahead of the rear wheels were Trans-Amesque air deflectors. There was pinstriping galore and a giant cartoonish Cobra decal on the hood, which, like that of the regular Cobra II, was rear-facing and non-functional. The coiled snake emblem was absent from the grille, and the head-light-trim rings were painted flat black, as were the window moldings, the windshield-wiper arms, taillight bezels, and wheels.

Hot Rod charitably called its engine, at a nearly impossible 139 horsepower (at 3,600 rpm), "spunky" and said that it was "the best-looking Mustang yet."

Sister publication *Car Craft* enlisted reigning Pro Stock champion "Dyno" Don Nicholson to wring one out at the drag strip. In its June 1978 issue, the magazine reported a best time of 17.06 at 80.69 mph with Dyno Don at the controls, "just a heartbeat quicker than the [Bob] Glidden-driven Pinto" that it had tested earlier. At least the 17.06 was an improvement over where Nicholson started the day—mid-17s at 78 mph.

A King Cobra Mustang cost almost $7,000, a huge piece of change in 1978, especially considering its dowdy performance.

The King Cobra option cost more than $1,200, but at least it included the heavy-duty suspension and 302 V8. Its array of decals, stripes, spoilers, and spats echoed those of Pontiac's successful Trans-Am.

Cobra II. Plus, the Pontiac could go around corners with the best of them; many magazines of the day crowned it the best-handling American car, better even than the much ballyhooed Corvette.

For 1977, Ford offered up the same basic package, though the Cobra II's stripes could now be had in red or green. The biggest news was the availability of removable glass T-roofs on the 2+2. They injected a bit of excitement into the line, and the television ads screamed, "Score Mustang II, Boredom 0." Also, the Cobra II front spoiler became a no-cost option on hatchback models. But it was in 1978 that things got a little weird in the Mustang II camp.

Despite its lack of performance, the Cobra II's graphics package stayed on the interesting side of tasteful. Not so in 1978. This would be the last year for the Mustang II, and Ford wanted to make certain that no one forgot it. No doubt influenced by the success of the special edition black-and-gold Trans-Ams, Ford put forward its gaudiest Cobra II yet. Stylists turned the previously front-facing hood scoop around, mimicking the T/A's rear-facing shaker. No big deal. Where things took a true turn for the unusual was in the graphics department. Gone were the traditional twice-stripes. In their place was a single flamboyant stripe that was almost as wide as the grille and ran the length of the car, up the front bumper, down the hood, across the roof, and down the deck lid and spoiler to the bumper. Instead of the relatively thin matching stripe that ran down the side rocker moldings, an extra-wide stripe covered the front fender, ran across the door (with the word "Cobra" in 12-inch or so letters), and extended all the way to the tail end of the rear fender. If you ordered the stripes in red, they were outlined in orange; if you

Opposite: Available for but one year, the King Cobra cost nearly $7,000, but couldn't run a sub 17-second quarter-mile. Above: The last year for the Mustang II (as well as the Cobra II and the Mach 1) was 1978. The Cobra II (pictured) now came with black window slats on the rear hatch glass, reminiscent of those used on the Boss 302 almost a decade earlier. A three-spoke steering wheel and brushed aluminum dash insert (left) added a more sporting nature to the Mustang II cockpit.

ordered blue, they were outlined in black. Also, the side-window moldings were painted a heavy flat black, as were the side-window louvers.

And this was the more subdued of the Cobra models. If you really wanted to get someone's attention—and hitting him in the head with a polo mallet wasn't an option—you ordered the King Cobra.

Perhaps Ford was onto something. Production for 1978 was up nearly 39,000 units, to 192,410. That was the second-best total for the Mustang II, and it helped the car retire on an up note. In the fall of 1978, Ford would introduce a completely redesigned Mustang based on its new Fox chassis. This new car would last longer than any previous Mustang and help usher in a second muscle-car era. In the process, it would become a cult vehicle, second only, perhaps, to the original ponycar.

As for the Mustang II, few people shed any tears when it disappeared. Enthusiasts today barely acknowledge it (if at all) as being a Mustang—a cruel fate, for, if nothing else, it kept the ponycar alive. The same cannot be said for its competition from Dodge, Plymouth, and American Motors. Gone are the Road Runners, Chargers, Super Bees, and Barracudas, probably forever. Without the Mustang II, there might not be a Mustang today.

Chapter Six

1979–1986
Fox on the Run

Because they were designed to provide relatively inexpensive transportation, all four generations of Mustangs to this day have been based on existing small-car platforms. The original's roots were in the lowly Falcon, a sturdy, if not spectacular, automobile. The Mustang came into the world at a time when Detroit's vision of what a car should be was all that mattered. There was little influence from outside forces on the big automobile companies. In fact, it wasn't until the Mustang's maiden year that seat belts became standard in American cars (and they could still be removed for credit). The Big Three—Ford, General Motors, and Chrysler—ruled supreme. When a GM executive said before the Senate that "what's good for General Motors is good for America," it was considered gospel.

By 1974, the rules had changed substantially. Detroit's behavior was closely monitored by environmentalists, the insurance industry, and the government. That triumvirate could easily have been called the Bigger Three. Ever-increasing government regulations added thousands to the sticker prices of new automobiles. Ford and its domestic competitors were dealt further staggering blows by the trio composed of OPEC, runaway inflation, and the Japanese automakers. War, famine, pestilence, and death had nothing on these guys.

Chrysler rekindled America's love affair with convertibles when it introduced the LeBaron ragtop in 1982 and it was only natural that the Mustang would be the car Ford used to re-enter the market in 1983. Ford sold a remarkable 23,438 convertibles that year. The '84 pictured wears the rare 20th anniversary GT350 paint/tape scheme.

Unfortunately for Ford fanciers, these outside influences forced unwelcome compromises on the Mustang II. Based on the Pinto, it was small, but heavy; emissions regulations and fuel-economy concerns choked every ounce of performance from its engines; 5-mph bumper crash standards made it look ungainly and detracted from its handling. Inflation also hurt. To keep the sticker price down while the costs of salaries and materials were sky-rocketing meant that Ford had to cheapen the product. Though the Mustang II sold fairly well, it probably didn't do much to inspire folks to return to their neighborhood Ford dealer at trade-in time.

For the third-generation Mustang, Ford engineers based the car on what was called the Fox platform. In 1978, Ford released the first Fox variants, the Ford Fairmont and Mercury Zephyr. They were designed to be inexpensive, yet reliable, small sedans. Certainly, they were simple, and, while largely forgotten today, they had a host of virtues. Enough, in fact, that the basic chassis lasted in the Mustang until 1993 and continues in heavily fortified form to this day. The current Mustang rides on what is known at Ford as the Fox-4 platform (the "4" stands for 1994, the year it was introduced).

While road testers in the enthusiast press didn't heap uncontrollable praise on the Fairmont/Zephyr twins, the cars were buoyed by their light weight and cavernous

While these three automobiles look very different, they are all based on the same "Fox" chassis shared with the Mustang. The Mercury Zephyr Z7 (top) and Ford Fairmont (center) were the first Fox-based cars and were introduced in the 1978 model year, while the '79 Capri (bottom) shed its European heritage and was now built on a U.S. assembly line as the Mustang's sister car.

engine bays. In its June 1978 issue, *Car Craft* tested a 302/four-speed-equipped Fairmont coupe and found it to be as fast as the Mustang II King Cobra. Not bad, considering that the King Cobra was driven by reigning Pro Stock world champ Don Nicholson. The stripped-down Fairmont's biggest benefit was that it weighed close to 500 pounds less than the Mustang II; that's the equivalent of roughly 50 free horsepower.

When the 1979 Mustang was introduced later that fall, it was blessed with the Fairmont's large engine compartment and light weight. Although it would be 1995 before Ford would use an engine larger than the 302 (now dubbed the 5-liter, owing to the metric system) in the Mustang, hot-rodders quickly learned that Ford's monstrous 460 V8 would drop in with few difficulties.

At the time of the '79 Mustang's introduction, Ford brought out a completely new Mercury Capri. Unlike previous "Sexy European" versions, this new Capri was all-American, mechanically a carbon copy of the Stang. Only front and rear styling and flared fenders separated the cars visually.

Both the Mustang and the Capri were available with three engines at first, all carryovers from the Mustang II. There was the 2.3L I-4, rated at 88 horsepower; the 2.8L V6 with 109 hp; and the 5.0L (302) V8, now rated at 139 ponies. Later in the model year, both cars got a boost from a turbocharged version of the four-banger that made 137 horsepower. It weighed less and actually allowed the smaller-engined car to run neck-and-neck with the V8. This was big news in 1979.

The front suspension on the new Stang was a revised MacPherson strut arrangement with the coil springs located low on the vertical struts; the rear featured four trailing arms, and there was a coil spring at each corner of the vehicle. The basic package handled ably and was free of vices, but enthusiasts were in for a real treat if they ordered the TRX tire/wheel/suspension package.

Developed around a set of 15.3-inch forged-aluminum wheels and 195/65R390 Michelin TRX elliptical radial tires, the package included special bushings, sway bars, shocks, struts, and springs. The difference in handling over stock was remarkable.

"In the handling department, at least, the TRX package does for the Mustang/Capri what the Trans-Am option does for Firebird," said a report in *Hot Rod*'s August 1978

issue. It praised the car's manners: "The steering and brakes—both borrowed from the Fairmont/Zephyr—are the best yet for a Mustang. The power-assisted, variable ratio, rack-and-pinion steering provides maximum effort and minimum ratio at the dead-center position; as the steering wheel is rotated, the effort decreases and the ratio increases."

The new styling shared virtually nothing with any Mustang that preceded it. The nose featured four rectangular headlights, which framed an egg crate–style grille. The nose was slanted back for better aerodynamics (the Mustang had a drag coefficient of 0.44, its lowest to date). Overall length was up 4.1 inches from 1978, to 179.1. The Mustang's wheelbase also increased, from 96.2 to 100.4 inches, creating more interior volume. Overall width decreased 3 inches, yet interior width actually increased from 52.5 inches of shoulder room to 56.1.

While the new car had a narrower width, it had a taller roofline, thus giving the Mustang a more vertical appearance. This was the opposite of any Stang before it (especially the '71–'73 versions) and was in stark contrast to the lower, longer, wider Firebirds and Camaros.

The Mustang came in two body styles, a two-door coupe with a traditional trunk, and a three-door hatch-

The all-new '79 Mustang was built in two body styles at first, a coupe (above) and a hatchback. For performance enthusiasts, both the 5.0 V8 (139 horsepower) and a turbo charged 2.3L four-cylinder engine (137 hp) were available. An aggressive ad campaign (right) helped sales jump from just over 192,000 in '78 to almost 370,000 in '79.

BACK HOME IN INDIANA—THE 1979 MUSTANG INDY PACE CAR

There are few sure-fire attention-getters in the automobile business, but one of the most successful is having a car named the pace car for the Indianapolis 500. Every year, manufacturers fight for the privilege; winning the battle means instant media coverage, both in print and on television. A live audience of 450,000 sees the car lead the pack in the most prestigious American race, with hundreds of millions more watching at home on television.

With a completely new Mustang in its stable for 1979, Ford wanted desperately to pace the big race. Its wish was granted. For the first time since 1964, a Mustang would pace the Indy 500. Naturally, a limited number of replicas would be built for sale in dealerships around the country.

The 1979 Pace Car was a very attractive automobile. The vehicles used at the actual race and their road-going cousins were virtually identical in looks. The body was a special pewter color with black striping on the hood and from the body-molding down. A red and orange stripe ran from the front fender back and up and over the roof. All carried the TRX handling package, and power came from either the 302 V8 or the 2.3L Turbo.

Inside, the Pace Car replicas used the same special Recaro sport seats as the actual pacers. There was also a simulated engine-turned instrument panel appliqué similar to the one used on that year's Cobra. Other optional features made standard on the Pace Cars were the leather-wrapped steering wheel, deluxe seat belts, and the console with graphic warning-display module and digital clock.

The Pace Car also came with a front air dam with integral fog lights, a rear spoiler (both of which would become optional on 1980 models), dealer- or owner-installed commemorative Indy Pace Car decals, a rear-facing hood scoop, and a pop-up sunroof. Unlike in 1964, when 36 were built, some 11,000 Pace Car replicas were built and were very popular at the time.

Somewhat overlooked today because of their lackluster acceleration, these pace cars are probably the most collectible of all the early (1979–1981) Fox Mustangs due to their unique appearance, unusual features, and pace car status.

Pace car Mustang replicas improved on an already stylish package with a revised front fascia that included a cowl hood, a large front air dam, and revised grille, among other features. And while the replicas didn't get the high-output engine (below) used in the Mustangs that actually paced the race, they are a good bet for future collectibility because of their limited production and Indy Pace Car status.

Had Ford listened to enthusiasts and supplied some serious horsepower in the Pace Car replicas, they would probably be worth a fortune today. The engine built to power the race's Mustang would have been perfect. Built by small-block Ford master Jack Roush, it had a heavy-duty, blueprinted block, Boss 302 forged-steel crank and connecting rods, TRW pistons, specially prepared 351-Windsor cylinder heads (1.84-inch intake valves, 1.54-inch exhaust), a Boss 302 cam, a dual-plane aluminum intake, and 600-cfm Holley four-barrel carb.

In other words, its powerful engine allowed Mustang to do the job at Indy. Even in smog-legal trim, it would have been potent enough to wrest the quickest-accelerating American car title away from the Corvette.

back that featured a fold-down rear seat. With the back-seat down, the Mustang's storage compartment was cavernous. As drag racers soon learned, you could carry drag slicks, tools, a floor jack, and just about anything else you might need for a day of racing. For budding families who wanted a little style, it was a perfect alternative to the station wagon.

While the new Mustang was perhaps not the sleekest ever (that distinction belongs to the fastbacks of the sixties), it was an instant smash with the buying public. Just under 370,000 Mustangs went out the door (369,936), along with 90,850 Capris. Ford obviously had another runaway success story to brag about, but it is doubtful that even the most optimistic executives dared to dream that this basic package would not only survive, but thrive until 1993.

1980 AND BEYOND

With the new Mustang, Ford offered hope to the die-hard enthusiasts who had been teased for years by graphics packages that suggested a wild ride. Thanks to the TRX suspension, the Mustang didn't lack for handling prowess. If it started, the Turbo 2.3 offered decent, but hardly earth-shattering, acceleration. Then Ford shattered its fans' dreams. It pulled the rug out from under them when it downsized the 5-liter engine to 4.2 liters (255 cubic inches). Instead of moving the Mustang forward, Dearborn engineers took one giant tumble backward. The new 4.2 barely managed 119 horsepower. When the turbocharged four-banger became unavailable in 1981, it left Stang Bangers without so much as a single weapon with which they could defend themselves in the high-performance jungle.

Fortunately, Ford began to redeem itself during the 1982 model year. The 5-liter V8 returned with a vengeance. The Mustang GT was reintroduced, and it packed a 157-horsepower promise. While this doesn't sound like much, it represented a startling improvement over anything that had been seen since 1973. Called the 5.0L H.O., the 302 now had a double-roller timing chain and a high-performance camshaft. Carburetion came via a large Holley two-barrel carb. Standard on the GT was a four-speed transmission and 3.08:1 Traction-Lok rear.

"The Boss Is Back," shouted the ads, and this time it wasn't just empty promises from Madison Avenue. The Mustang GT actually delivered the goods. While it didn't have the sex appeal of the gorgeous new Camaro introduced that year (or the handling prowess), it could run away from the Chevy in the acceleration department.

In its March 1982 issue, *Motor Trend* brought these two archrivals together for a head-to-head shoot-out. Heralding the cover story as "Power vs. Precision," the editors flogged the pair at Willow Springs Raceway, north of Los Angeles. The Camaro, powered by a 305-four-barrel V8 and backed by a five-speed transmission, proved superior on the road course and held a distinct advantage in 60–0 mph braking. When it came to acceleration, however, the new Mustang GT burst away from its nemesis, besting it in 0–60 acceleration (7.78 vs. 8.58 seconds) and in the quarter mile (16.26/83.70 vs. 16.67/81.00 for the Chevy).

As far as looks were concerned, the '82 GT had a lot going for it. A bold air dam with integrated fog lights, slatted grille, and forward-facing hood scoop made it look mean, while a deck lid spoiler added a nice touch out back. Exciting options were the TRX handling/suspension package, Recaro seats, and T-roofs.

While low 16-second quarters wouldn't let you choose off Cross-Fire-injected Corvettes, the '82 GTs were dubbed modern muscle cars, thanks to their computer controls

"The Boss Is Back." So trumpeted Ford's print ads in 1982, and the 5.0L H.O. engine offered a significant increase in horsepower for the first time in years. Ford brought back the GT model (opposite) for the first time since 1969, and the 5.0 H.O. was standard. Also included in the GT package were the front and rear spoilers first seen on the Indy Pace Car three years earlier and the popular TRX wheel, tire, and suspension setup.

Forcepower—The Turbocharged Mustang, Part One

In the horsepower-starved time of the late 1970s, any engine that even remotely promised a good time was cause for a celebration. Such was the case with Ford's first production-turbocharged power plant, the in-line 2.3L Four. When word leaked out that this upcoming force-fed engine could deliver V8 power with four-cylinder fuel economy and clean emissions, it created quite a stir.

A turbocharger is an exhaust-driven supercharger. Inside the turbo housing is a turbine, which is spun by exhaust gases. Once the turbine starts spinning, it forces compressed air back into the intake system. Think of the engine as little more than an air pump. The more air that it pumps, the more power it makes. With properly matched fuel and ignition systems, a turbocharger can boost an engine's power by 100 percent or more. In the case of the 2.3, horsepower increased from 88 to 132, or almost one horsepower per cubic inch of displacement.

Ford, of course, wasn't the only manufacturer experimenting with turbos. Porsche made the world stand up and take notice with its powerful 911 Turbo (known as the 930), the fastest vehicle on the planet in 1976. On the domestic front, Oldsmobile had offered a production-turbo option as early as 1962 on its Jetfire sport coupe. That car's tiny 215-inch V8 received a much needed shot in the arm with the addition of the optional Turbo-Rocket, making 215 horsepower and 310 foot-pounds of torque. But with premium fuel selling for about a quarter a gallon, it was easier to build larger engines than add an expensive, high-tech piece like a turbo.

In the mid- and late seventies, however, GM reached back into its technology bank and once again began exploring the feasibility of using turbos on everything from Corvettes to family sedans. At first, only Buick offered production-turbo models, the Regal and LeSabre. Turbocharged Pontiac Grand Prix and Trans-

A variety of turbocharged four-cylinder engines would appear under the hood of the Fox Mustang from 1979 to 1986 and while they were capable performers, they proved troublesome as well. The strongest was the 175-horse 2.3L in the '86 SVO.

Ams, Chevy Monte Carlos, and even pickup trucks would come later.

For the most part, GM stuck to V6 applications. Ford, for reasons unknown, decided to try turbocharging on the 2.3L Four. This meant that it had to be substantially beefed up to cope with the rigors of the turbo. Both rod and main bearings were upgraded, and a set of TRW forged pistons were mandated with special rings. Intake and exhaust valves were upgraded to cope with the higher temperatures that were created by the turbo, and a solid-steel-core head gasket was used as well. Naturally, the oiling system was also improved.

The turbo was an AiResearch T03 model with a built-in waste gate that started bleeding off boost at 5 psi and everything over 6 psi. A two-barrel Holley carb fed the fuel via an aluminum intake manifold, and the mixture was fired by an electronic ignition that was designed to retard the timing under boost. (This keeps the engine from experiencing harmful pre-ignition or detonation—most commonly known as "pinging.")

Increased cooling capacity kept the engine from overheating, and a very steep (for the era) 3.45:1 final drive ratio helped make up for the small engine's inherent lack of low-end torque. Combined with its lighter weight (about 2,550 pounds), the Turbo Mustang could accelerate as well as a V8 model. Both could cover the quarter mile in about 16.7 seconds at about 81 mph—not as fast as the strongest Trans-Ams and Z/28s, but a huge improvement over any Mustang dating back to 1974.

Unfortunately, reliability—or lack thereof—became an immediate issue with Ford's 2.3L turbo, and the company pulled it from the market after the 1980 model year. A 2.3L Turbo GT model would return in 1983, this time with 145 hp, and the much heralded Mustang SVO, with 175 horses, would arrive the following year.

and, later on, fuel injection. This was the dawning of the second muscle-car era. So impressive was the Mustang GT's performance that the California Highway Patrol purchased 400 of these bad boys for high-speed pursuit duty. This Special Service Package became so popular that over the next eleven years, thirty-five states and more than 100 sheriffs' departments drafted the 5-liter Mustang for police work. Though the Special Service Package was dropped after the '93 model year, many states, including California, refuse to banish these ponies to the glue factory. They continue to refurbish them and send them out after speeders.

For 1983, Ford chucked the two-barrel carb and made a genuine 600-cfm four-barrel Holley standard on the GT. Mustang lovers rejoiced. Now breathing through a dual-snorkel air filter and pumping out 175 horses, the new GT was the fastest Mustang since the Boss 351 of 1971 and was capable of high 6-second 0–60 times and mid-to-low 15-second ETs at the drags.

There was plenty of other good news for 1983. The Mustang received its first major nose job, making it appear somewhat sleeker and more aerodynamic. The GT's hood scoop was reversed, and there were new tail lamps as well. Handling was bolstered by larger, 220-millimeter-wide tires if you ordered the TRX suspension. Best of all, after a ten-year hiatus, a genuine, fun-in-the-sun convertible returned to the lineup, giving the prospective buyer a choice of three distinct body styles—coupe, hatchback, or ragtop.

Convertibles received additional chassis bracing to make up for the integrity lost when the roof got cut off and a genuine glass rear window was used. The turbo four-cylinder engine returned, now with electronic fuel injection, but the fast ride delivered by the 5.0's prodigious torque made it superfluous.

This time, it was *Car and Driver*'s turn to heap praise on the pony. In a comparison with the '83 Camaro Z/28 5.0 H.O. in its June 1983 issue, the new Mustang GT measured a 0–60 time of 7 seconds flat and a quarter-mile time of 15.4 seconds at 90 mph—nearly a full second and 7 mph faster in the quarter than an '82 GT.

"In sum, the Mustang builds up to its limits very quickly, and in a fashion the citizen driver can use to excellent advantage....If you like low-speed stunt driving accompanied by clouds of tire smoke, the Mustang GT gets it," the magazine stated.

Refinement was the key word for 1984. After undergoing a fairly substantial revamping twelve months earlier, Ford engineers worked to fine-tune the Mustang's behavior. An 8.8-inch rear replaced the spindly 7.5-incher used earlier, a move dictated by the Mustang's ever-increasing horsepower. A Quadra-Shock suspension system—two vertical shocks and two horizontal shocks—was employed to curtail dreaded wheel hop, as well as to keep the rear planted during hard cornering maneuvers.

Changes to the engines were minimal. The Turbo GT returned virtually a carryover, as did the four-barrel 5.0 GT—unless you ordered the new automatic-overdrive transmission. If you did, you got a throttle-body fuel-injection system (called CFI, for Central Fuel Injection) that sapped 10 horsepower from the engine.

The biggest news for 1984 was the introduction of the twentieth-anniversary model and the high-performance Mustang SVO. While the twentieth-anniversary car was basically a tape stripe package (red stripes on a white body and GT350 lettering on the doors), the SVO was a genuine effort by Ford to build a BMW-beater, a high-tech machine that combined V8-type performance (but without a V8 engine), a unique appearance, excellent handling, and exclusivity.

Its name derived from Ford's then-new Special Vehicle Operations, the group responsible for engineering it. Power came from a turbocharged four-cylinder engine, but it wasn't the same pot that was used in the Turbo GT. This engine was exclusive to the SVO. Still displacing

Above: T-tops were still available on the GT in 1983, but the big news was under the hood. A genuine Holley four-barrel carburetor helped boost horsepower to 175, which knocked nearly a second from the quarter-mile time. Still, the price remained under $10,000, at $9,449.

Following page: The 1984 SVO Mustang differed from the Mustang GT in many ways, including the flush grille with single headlights, 16-inch wheels with Goodyear NCT tires, the rear quarter glass treatment, and biplane rear spoiler.

2.3L, the SVO's heart had an air-to-air intercooler and electronic fuel injection, thus boosting horsepower to 175—the same as the V8 in the GT. The front suspension was revised and featured Koni adjustable struts; there were also reworked springs, front and rear stabilizer bars, four-wheel disc brakes, a Quadra-Shock rear suspension, and 16-by-7-inch wheels with Goodyear 225/50 Goodyear NCT tires.

The cockpit featured a special leather-wrapped three-spoke steering wheel, unique instrument panel and seats, plus a left-foot dead pedal with which the driver could brace himself under high cornering loads.

Best of all, the SVO looked like no other Mustang. Found only on the SVO were a functional scooped hood, which ducted air to the intercooler; large, single rectangular headlights; a revamped front fascia; special tail lamps; 16-inch wheels; a bi-plane rear spoiler; side spats in front of the rear wheels; and cleaner side-window moldings.

Except for excess engine vibrations, the SVO was a fairly refined package, offering excellent balance and performance. There were just two problems: potential BMW buyers were about as likely to buy a Mustang as they were a used Pinto. Also, the 5-liter Mustang GT kept getting better and offered the same, if not better, performance for thousands of dollars less. When the SVO was conceived, it was believed that the V8 engine was a dinosaur soon to be extinct. Luckily for car enthusiasts, when the real dinosaurs died, they spent the next few million years becoming oil—hence the term "fossil fuels." Technology helped big-inch V8s become more efficient than ever, and with the price of gas spiraling downward, the thrill of a torquey American muscle engine proved irresistible for many buyers.

By 1985, the 5-liter H.O. was making 210 horsepower (the SVO got bumped to 205), thanks in part to a set of genuine tube headers and a more efficient belt-drive system for the accessories. The Fox Mustang also received another face-lift, its grille now somewhat reminiscent of the SVO, but with four headlights. Those purchasing the GT with an automatic overdrive transmission once again got shortchanged—to the tune of 45 horsepower. They were still saddled with the 165-hp CFI engine.

Fans of the SVO reveled in the glory of a 30-horsepower increase as well, thanks to an increase in turbo boost (from 14 psi to 15), a revised camshaft, a freer-flow-

You didn't have to buy a GT to get the hot 5-liter engine. This '84 hatchback has the TRX suspension package, but a more subtle appearance without the GT's blacked-out hood and scoop.

MUSTANG SVO: RIGHT CAR, WRONG TIME

No good deed goes unpunished. How true this proved to be in the case of the high-performance Mustang SVO. Ford's engineers had a genuine desire to build a lightweight, technologically advanced, eco-conscious canyon carver for the latter part of the twentieth century. While their hearts and minds were in the right place, the market changed almost overnight.

Ford's Special Vehicle Operations group consisted of twenty-eight people, according to the print ad they ran in the enthusiast press at the time, and their mission was to produce a European-style, grand touring automobile that relied on high technology rather than brute force for its greatness. That meant no gas-guzzling V8 engine, and an ergonomically correct and friendly cockpit that allowed the driver to concentrate on the business at hand. It meant exclusivity (and therefore, a higher price) and placing a premium on design innovation and style.

Little touches unheard of in previous Mustangs were the norm, for instance, the throttle, clutch, and brake

They called the '84–86 Mustang SVO the "high-tech hot rod" and with good reason. It was powered by a fuel-injected, turbocharged, four-cylinder engine that made power like a V8. It also offered excellent handling and features such as adjustable clutch, brake, and throttle pedals. The SVO interior also had multi-adjustable sport seats that offered support equal to the car's handling.

pedals were repositioned for optimum heel-and-toe driving. Expensive Goodyear NCT tires and a genuine Hurst shifter were standard, where lesser rubber and a flaccid factory shifter would have sufficed earlier. Multi-adjustable, special seats actually suited to spirited driving were designed and made standard. Body cladding,

flush wheels, and the biplane rear spoiler seemed more suited to Ford of Europe's high-zoot Sierra models.

The turbocharged four-cylinder engine met the needs of engineers who were looking for a small, light mill that could be modified to make power, but it proved too harsh in actual use and didn't fit with the sophistication of the rest of the car. Its thrashiness ultimately turned off a number of buyers, even after it had been massaged to make 205 horsepower, thanks to an increase in boost, revised camshaft, and a better exhaust system.

When it was introduced in mid-1984, it was greeted warmly by the press. Available in red, black, charcoal, and silver, the Mustang SVO exhibited refined road manners and offered plenty of grip. Magazines sang its praises, but ultimately, few buyers warmed up to its robust price of $15,277. It seems that Mustang buyers want a car that is slightly crude and ill-mannered. While the SVO suffered, sales of the GT and other 5-liter-powered Mustangs soared.

Model Year	SVO Production	5-Liter Production
1984	4,508	38,194
1985	1,954	48,754
1986	3,382	57,139

In addition to the engine upgrades mentioned above, the SVO benefited from a few other changes for 1985. Flush headlights purified the look of the front end, and the use of different engine brackets allowed less of the four banger's ruckus to make its way into the cabin. The steering ratio was reduced to 14.7:1, and Teflon-lined stabilizer-bar bushings, tauter shocks, and Goodyear Eagle tires contributed to improved handling. But some of the SVO's features, like its steering wheel and Quadra-Shock rear, were also available on the GT.

By 1986, the gig was pretty much up for this warrior. It was a noble experiment, but with the 5-liter's performance so thrilling for far less money, it became superfluous. Also, the price of fuel had tumbled from the beginning of the decade and its supply stabilized. People were no longer fearful of bigger engines and thus sales of temperamental four-cylinder turbos dwindled accordingly.

ing exhaust system, larger fuel injectors, and a reworked intake manifold. The suspension was upgraded with stiffer shocks and struts, quicker steering, and Goodyear Eagle tires.

The most significant news for 1985 was that this would be the last year that buyers could purchase a carbureted V8 Mustang. For '86, both automatic and five-speed GTs would receive a multiport sequential fuel-injection system, which greatly increased low-end torque, horsepower, and drivability. Horsepower was down to 200 because of a change in cylinder heads, but this would be the last time for many years that Mustang enthusiasts would gripe about horsepower. The following year saw a genuine explosion in performance. The Mustang was about to become the most sought-after automobile for an entire new generation of muscle-car enthusiasts.

The Mustang received another facelift in 1985. An all-new grille arrived, as did different side moldings. It would be the final year for the carbureted 5-liter engine; sequential electronic fuel injection arrived in 1986.

CHAPTER SEVEN

1987–1993
LONG LIVE THE KING

Against all odds, muscle cars rushed back to the forefront of the American scene in the late eighties. Horsepower, for years a word spoken in hushed tones, was being shouted from the rooftops of every building in Motor City. Advertisements that only a few years earlier bespoke fuel economy and environmental friendliness now blazed with burning rubber, 0–60 times, and thrills that only high performance could deliver.

Maybe the newfound popularity of the muscle cars was the ultimate expression of the feel-good Reagan years. New Detroit iron delivered the goods as it had in the sixties, but this time it did so with a social conscience—clean tailpipe emissions and gas mileage that had previously been reserved for Japanese eco-boxes became the norm.

By the '87 model year, Ford had scrapped the Capri and was dedicating the bulk of its performance dollars to V8 Mustang development. This meant the end of the line for the much-revered SVO. Thanks to a revised 5-liter engine, the Mustang stole the hearts of performance enthusiasts weaned on sixties supercars and won converts from both the GM and Chrysler camps.

The Mustang underwent wholesale changes in 1987. Front and rear styling were new, borrowing heavily from the SVO. Large, single rectangular headlights (now flush with the grille) and a blunt nose gave the beast a more con-

The evil-looking '87 Mustang GT (pictured) bore a striking resemblance to the now-departed SVO. A large front air dam with integrated fog lights, side skirts, a large rear valance, and louvered taillights made up much of the GT's styling package. Thanks to its 225-horse engine, it took a back seat to no one when it came to performance.

temporary look. The tail lamps were modified slightly, and the side-glass trim was simplified for a more sanitary look.

If you ordered a GT, you got the wildest-looking Fox Mustang yet. A large front air dam, rear wing, and side skirts with air ducts and turbine-style wheels gave the GT a bold appearance (not to mention two-tone paint at no extra cost). Out back, the unusual louvered taillights never failed to draw comment. For years (dating back to the early sixties), Pontiac had experimented, especially on Trans-Ams, with different treatments to make the taillights disappear, which gave the cars a bit of a custom look. The GT's "cheese grater" taillights, while appearing overblown to some, fit perfectly with the car's image.

The interior was totally revamped—patterned, some said, on the BMW 3 series. It was certainly more European than American. The instruments were housed in a single pod rather than individual binnacles, the controls were placed more logically, and the passenger side of the dash was less intrusive, giving the cabin an airy feel.

The real story of the '87 Mustang was under the hood. Revised cylinder heads (actually the ones previously used in Ford's 5-liter truck engines) and a larger throttle body helped boost horsepower from 200 to 225 and torque from 285 foot-pounds to 300. More important than the actual numbers, though, is how the cars performed. Available in the GT and the much lighter, downscale LX,

the 5-liter-equipped Stangs were beasts. Fuel injection and computer controls helped boost low-speed performance, providing stump-pulling torque. This, combined with the Mustang's 3,100-pound (or thereabouts) curb weight, allowed the '87s to turn in performance figures commensurate with some of the big-block Mustangs of the sixties.

Cars Illustrated, a now-defunct magazine, tested two 5-liter LX Mustangs. The first, a black hatchback without air conditioning or a radio, ran 13.7s; the second, a maroon hatchback with more options (including air conditioning), ran 14.0s at 99 mph. Remarkably, these times were achieved on stock street radials, which offered little traction. A third LX, a project car for *Super Stock & Drag Illustrated*, set an IHRA Pure Stock ET record. Buoyed in part by the exploits of these three giant-killers, buyers broke down the doors at Ford dealerships, helping V8 Mustang sales increase from 57,139 in 1986 to 64,148 in 1987. According to Al Kirschenbaum's *V8 Mustang Specifications Guide*, sales would peak at 105,577 in 1989—meaning that more than half of all Mustangs sold that year were of the high-performance variety.

Was it sheer balls-to-the-wall acceleration that made the cars so popular? Not really, for they had a host of other virtues. While not as up-to-date from an engineering standpoint as competitors from GM and overseas, the 5-liter Mustangs were simple to work on. They were also reliable and much less expensive than the Camaro Z/28 and Firebird Trans-Am and Formula. Plus, the word on the street was out—these engines liked to be tweaked. Simple tricks like increasing the initial timing and removing the air silencer in the intake tract could result in gains of about 20–25 horsepower. Suddenly, it was 1965 all over again, and kids from fifteen to fifty-five wanted a piece of the action.

CAN THE HORSE SURVIVE?

There were, believe it or not, dark clouds on the Mustang's horizon, despite its reemergence as a strong player in the marketplace. It seems that no one was more surprised by the 5-liter Stang's success than Ford's engineers and marketing executives. Even while the new 5.0s were kicking asphalt at drag strips across the United

The Mustang LX offered one of the best values on the market back in 1987. A four-cylinder convertible cost just $13,052, and was still under $15,000 with the 5-liter V8. Back in 1991 and 1992, the SAAC Car Company, an arm of the Shelby American Automobile Club, offered the SAAC MK 1 (right), MK 2, and SAAC Snake, a specially prepared series of high-performance Mustangs. All MK 1s were hatchbacks painted white with blue stripes and were available only to members of the club. The MK 2 was also available as a convertible and available to the general public. Both came standard with a 295-horse, EPA-legal, 5-liter engine. The Snake had all the features of the MK 1 and MK2 without the special engine (below). Following Page: The last year for the turbine wheels on the GT was 1989 (pictured). They would be replaced with a more modern five-spoke wheel in 1990. Convertible GTs were popular, though heavier than the coupes, and were prone to body flex.

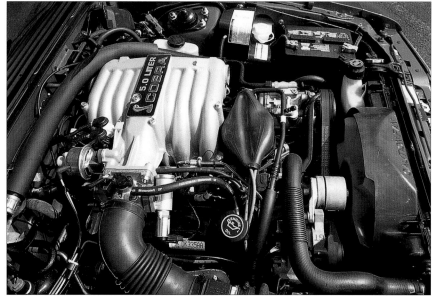

Opposite: Though 1993 was the last of a 15-year model run for the Fox Mustang, Ford sent it away with a very special model, the Cobra. It came standard with a less harsh, but grippier suspension, an underrated 235-horsepower engine, and unique wheels, tires, and body appearance package. The Cobra engine featured a set of GT-40–style cylinder heads, a cast-aluminum GT-40 intake (versus the tubular aftermarket version), unique accessory pulleys, and 1.7:1 ratio rocker arms to boost horsepower. Below: By the early 1990s, modified Mustangs were quickly becoming the car of choice for drag racers from coast to coast.

States and Canada, plans were being readied to discontinue the V8, rear-drive Mustang and replace it with a smaller, four- or six-cylinder-powered front-wheel-drive vehicle that was—gasp!—co-engineered by Mazda. The thought of an all-American ponycar sharing its chassis and engine with Japanese sports coupes and sedans was more than the traditionally "Buy American"–biased Mustang lovers would stand for. When word of this got out to the general public, Ford was overwhelmed with letters and phone calls from outraged Mustang enthusiasts.

Though things stopped short of a public lynching, the outcry was so great that it was decided to continue the Fox Mustang until a rear-drive replacement could be readied in 1994. As for the front driver, that project was too far along to kill. Ford would rename it the Probe and introduce it as a 1989 model. The Probe succeeded quite well, though it never did outsell the Mustang.

But a Japanese-American Mustang was a close call. Ford executives noted later that there were actually future Probes running around the proving grounds in Dearborn with "Mustang" badges on them.

As the decade wore on, there were few changes in store for the Mustang. The T-roof disappeared after only a handful of cars were built with this option in 1988.

Though popular, the roof panels were prone to squeaks, rattles, and water leaks. The disappearance of this option mattered little to the faithful Mustang buyer, however. Despite the fact that there were more advanced and more practical cars for sale, the Mustang's popularity soared. A total of 211,225 cars flooded the streets that year, with another 209,769 sold in 1989. Thanks to the easing of a silly regulation, the car's useless 85-mph speedometer was replaced with a more practical (and accurate) 140-mph unit.

In 1990, the Mustang received a driver's-side airbag. To offset the cost of retooling (Ford was milking this puppy for all it was worth), the optional tilt steering wheel was discontinued. Also, the first of a series of limited-edition LX convertibles appeared midway through the model year. The first was deep emerald metallic green with a white interior. In 1992, 2,019 vibrant red/white ragtops were sold, and in 1993, Ford offered two more options. One was bright yellow with a white leather interior and chromed five-spoke wheels (1,503 built); the other was all white, right down to the wheels (1,500 built).

Speculation about the next-generation ponycar abounded in the early nineties. While it was enjoying a great revival, the body and chassis had been around for

Two limited-edition Mustang convertibles were offered in 1993: one was yellow with a white interior and chrome rims, while the other was all white, including the rims.

over a decade, and to some, it was getting a bit stale. In head-to-head comparisons, the Fox chassis was starting to show its age.

Still, the ponycar was not about to go down without a few final flourishes. In 1990, Chevrolet introduced a special lightweight IROC-Z Camaro called the 1LE. The stripped-down package had a road-race suspension, five-speed transmission, and a 225-horse Tuned Port Injected 305-inch small-block (335 foot-pounds of torque). To find out if a specially prepared Chevy could beat a stock LX, *Muscle Mustangs & Fast Fords* brought the duo together for a shoot-out in its September 1990 issue. Despite having less torque and numerically lower gears, the lighter LX prevailed in the best-two-out-of-three battle, running a best of 14.29/97.08 to the Camaro's 14.46/96.60.

Three years later, Ford's Special Vehicle Team (SVT), the spiritual successor to the defunct SVO group, prepared a remarkable top-of-the-line Mustang. Its suspension was tweaked for a more compliant ride, yet it offered better handling than the GT. The body got a special open grille, unique ground effects, and rear wing, plus SVO-style taillights. Extra-large 17-inch rims carried beefy P245/45ZR Goodyear tires and hid four-wheel disc brakes.

Under the hood was a hot-rodder's dream. The 5-liter engine was fitted with some of the hottest parts from the Ford hi-po catalogue, including a cast version of the company's after-market GT-40 intake and GT-40-style cylinder heads, a different camshaft, and 1.7:1-ratio rocker arms (to give the cam more lift). Purposely underrated at 235 horsepower, actual output was in the neighborhood of 270 ponies. Ford called it the Cobra.

Available in red, black, or metallic teal, the Cobra's mission was to provide premium transportation for a very limited number of buyers. Except for the driving position, which was still hampered by the lack of an adjustable steering wheel, the Cobra met or exceeded all its goals.

To steal some of Chevrolet's thunder, Ford introduced the latest Cobra around the same time that its rival was unveiling its first new Camaro in eleven years. The new Camaro, once again called the Z/28, had much in its favor—four-wheel disc brakes, a six-speed transmission, and a 275-horsepower version of the Corvette's LT1 engine. On paper, it didn't look like the Cobra could compete.

The reality was something different. *Muscle Mustangs & Fast Fords* and its sister publication, *MuscleCars*, hosted

1993 COBRA R

Ford's Special Vehicle Engineering group, in an effort to make the Mustang more competitive in showroom stock-style racing, built a limited number of (race only) model "R" Cobras in 1993. Motivation for the R came from the same power train as the standard Cobra, but there were some noteworthy differences.

For starters, neither a radio nor a rear seat was available. All sound deadening was removed. Four-wheel disc brakes became standard, and larger PBR disc-brake calipers were employed up front.

Unlike the standard Cobras, which had a softer ride than that of the standard GT, the R models rode like trucks. And without a rear seat, the interior took on the din of an empty oil drum. Though they met all government standards for safety, fuel economy, and emissions, these were definitely not designed for street prowling.

A mere 107 Cobra Rs were built in 1993, and most of them were, to the disappointment of Ford engineers, snapped up by collectors and speculators. Few ever turned a hot lap in anger on a racetrack. The price was $25,217, but many sold for well beyond sticker.

Even though the '93 Cobra Rs never made a name for themselves on the track, their existence helped make standard many necessary parts for all Fox Mustangs. It also taught Ford a few lessons about what was needed to win races—like more power and greater fuel capacity. When Ford decided to build another Cobra R in 1995, it would be a much improved vehicle.

The rarest and most significant '93 Mustang was the Cobra R model. It came with the standard 235-horse Cobra engine and a harsh, race-only suspension. Such niceties as a radio, backseat, power windows, and air conditioning were not available.

IT TAKES ONE TO CATCH ONE

As Fox Mustang production wound down in 1993, another interesting piece of ponycar history went away with it—the Special Service Package Mustang. Designed as a high-speed pursuit vehicle for police, it became a victim of the trend toward high horsepower in all models. The SSP Mustang was born out of the need by law-enforcement agencies for a capable pursuit vehicle. As factory horsepower tumbled in the late 1970s and early 1980s, the typical cop car was a 4,500-pound barge with barely enough horsepower to get rolling. It became increasingly difficult for the full-sized and even the mid-sized police cruisers to meet the performance criteria established by departments across the country. In simple terms, the cops couldn't catch a rolling doughnut in one of these things. This lack of performance often put the lives of officers in danger.

They couldn't merge into traffic or apprehend suspects, and the cars didn't handle well at high speeds and couldn't brake from them. The Mustang's high-speed capabilities enabled police departments to address these inadequacies, as well as to do away with the dangerous practice of using two separate vehicles—a radar car and a flagman up ahead—to catch speeders. This practice had meant that police officers were sometimes run over or hit as they attempted to pull over the alleged offender.

What made up the Special Service Package? The main differences were not under the hood. Basically, the car was fortified for rigorous duty, with heavier-duty alternators, upgraded cooling systems, a calibrated 160-mph speedometer, a reinforced floor pan, and the like. Both the 5-speed (3.08 gears) and automatic overdrive (2.73 gears) were available.

Not exactly what the leadfoot Mustang owner wants to see in his rearview mirror. Born out of the need for a capable pursuit vehicle, the Special Service Package Mustang is now reaching cult status among collectors and enthusiasts.

Mustang Special Service Package featured:

Air deflector, front lower radiator

Remote deck-lid release relocated to the right of the steering column

Metal disc-brake rotor shields

External engine-oil cooler

Reinforced front floor pan (both sides)

Aircraft-type radiator and heater-hose clamps

Single-key locking system

Automatic-transmission oil cooler

Restrictor for the heater-hose inlet

Heavy-duty front seats

Calibrated 160-mph speedometer (in 2-mph increments)

Full-size spare tire and wheel

Under-hood sound deadener removed

Any of the Mustang's regular production options, such as air conditioning and power windows, were available on the SSP cars. Also available were Limited Production Options (LPO)—a front license-plate bracket and a 600-watt engine-block heater—and Dealer Special Orders (DSO)—a 135-amp alternator, silicone hoses with special clamps, inoperative-door courtesy-light switches, front-door molding delete, paint stripes delete, radio-noise-suppression package police radio, and a VASCAR speedometer cable.

Approximately 15,000 SSP Mustangs were assembled from 1982 to 1993, and except for (maybe) one '82 hatchback, all were built on the notchback body.

So why doesn't Ford offer an SSP Mustang if it proved so popular? There is less of a need for them now. The Crown Victoria, with the new 200-plus horsepower 4.6L Romeo V8, offers enough performance. The Crown Vics meet or exceed all applicable standards, so Ford management considers an SSP Mustang superfluous.

Still, though officers sometimes complained about the Mustang's cramped cabin (packed with radios, radar, and VASCAR equipment; there was barely enough room for one passenger), a large number of SSP ponies are still serving as law-enforcement vehicles.

The Mustang Mach III show car gave the motoring public a hint of what the next-generation Mustang would look like. Among the cues were the three-spoke wheels, three-bar taillights, open-mouth grille, and dual-cockpit interior.

shoot-outs between the Cobra and the Z/28. The results were a shock. Despite an apparent 40-horsepower disadvantage, the Cobra ran a 13.75 at 98.27 mph. The Camaro ran a 13.88 at 99.19 before succumbing to a case of bad fuel. Before the day was out, the Cobra, which weighed 150 pounds less than the Chevy, even though it was laden with a leather interior and every available option, ran a 13.47/100.81 with slicks, a short accessory drive belt, and bumped timing. This was truly a stout automobile.

As a top-of-the-line automobile, the Cobra was a heckuva Mustang. It came with all the right equipment, and the numbers proved it. What the numbers couldn't show, however, was just what a blast the Cobra was to drive. Its engine was always willing, and it pulled like no 5.0 before it. Plus, the suspension was infinitely more compliant. Though a bit too soft for some, it was the ultimate Fox-chassis car to that point.

Sales of the standard LX and GT models began slipping as the nineties wore on. Their 5-liter engine had been down-rated to 205 horsepower. Ford claimed that this was the result of changes over the past few years, which had eaten up a few ponies here and there. Also, it claimed that its new rating system more accurately reflected true output.

Cynics, on the other hand, thought that it was only a paper change designed to make 1994's all-new model with 215 horsepower—10 less than previous Mustangs—seem more palatable.

CHAPTER EIGHT

1994–1996
GALLOPING INTO THE
TWENTY-FIRST CENTURY

W hen Ford announced in the late 1980s that the Mustang would soldier on as a front-engined, rear-wheel-drive platform, Mustang fanatics were relieved and overjoyed. Their favorite car would stay true to its American heritage and power-train layout. But what would a Mustang facing the twenty-first century be like?

Some hoped a high-output version of the 5-liter's big brother, the 351 (now known in metric-speak as the 5.8L) would be available to combat Chevrolet's powerful 350 in the Z/28. There were strong rumblings that a fortified version of the Lincoln Mark VIII's dual-overhead-cam 4.6L V8 making 300 (or more) horsepower would appear. Others clamored for the single-overhead-cam 4.6. And, as hard as it was to believe, some people were ready to shove the venerable 5.0 aside. This engine, which had not only saved Ford high performance but had come to define it, might just be put out to pasture.

What would the new car look like? What gearbox would it have? Would it be smaller and lighter? Lower, wider, longer? Heavier? For years leading up to its actual release, the 1994 Mustang was the subject of much conjecture, hypothesizing, argument, and fist pounding. And why not? The Mustang is one of the automotive world's great nameplates, probably the most important American car after the Corvette. It has generated one of the most

The 1994 Mustang convertible featured a host of improvements, including a better-sealing top, reduced interior noise, and less turbulence with the top down. Most importantly, its structure was substantially stiffer. Also, the convertible top was lined, which not only helped keep out the cold in winter, but made it seem more expensive, more finished.

fiercely loyal and protective followings on the planet. It inspires passion in its drivers, not least because of its long and storied history of racing and visual exitement.

The just-released GM ponycar twins, Camaro and Firebird, had raised the ante substantially. They offered supercar handling, muscle-car acceleration, wild looks, and outstanding features for about $17,000. Similarly equipped, they were actually cheaper than the vehicles that they replaced. Combined with such goodies as a six-speed transmission and a 275-horse engine (standard on the Z/28 and Firebird Formula and Trans-Am), the new Mustang was arousing more expectations than any Stang that preceded it.

So when Ford delivered a GT with only 215 horses, the same five-speed transmission that it had had before, controversial styling, and a much higher price tag, many Mustang lovers felt betrayed.

Not that the new Mustang was a bad car—it was an excellent package—but the faithful wanted more.

Ford spent $700 million revamping the Fox Mustang, which seems like a lot, but actually isn't for this kind of undertaking. Engineers cut a lot of corners to bring the '94 in for so little. That meant that much of the earlier Mustang remained. The 5-liter engine, which actually lost some ponies because of its revised intake tract (necessitated so that the engine would fit under the lower hood

line), was virtually a carryover from '93, as was the T-5 tranny and 8.8-inch rear. The automatic transmission was an electronic version of the AOD, known as the AOD-E.

The chassis, though substantially fortified, was still based on the Fox platform that dated back to the '78 Fairmont. It was now called Fox-4.

Most of the development money was spent on three areas: retooling, redesigning the interior, and new body-work. The Mustang would continue to be built in only one factory, the Dearborn assembly plant. Ford's oldest, the plant once produced Model Ts.

As for the interior, it was virtually new and perhaps the best part of the new Mustang. It bore a striking resemblance to Ford's 1993 Mach III showcar and the '63–'67 Corvette Sting Rays. It was a styling tour de force, a dual-cockpit theme with semicircular pods. The one in front of the driver housed all the essential instruments—directly in the driver's line of sight—behind a proper four-spoke steering wheel. Happily, the tilt feature had returned and was now standard equipment. The radio, heater, and the controls for ventilation and air conditioning (HVAC) were mounted in the center of the dash, all within easy reach of the driver. A center console with a storage compartment and armrest was standard, as were airbags for the driver and the passenger.

Styling also strongly resembled the Mach III. Though that vehicle was built as a two-seater, its open grille, hood line, taillights, and (once again) C-shaped side indentation all screamed '94 Mustang. (If you listened closely, its wheels would say '96 GT.) From the rear, the '94 GT looked chopped off, with an incredibly high bustle. Also, its ride height was way too high. There was so much room between the tops of the tires and the fender wells that some said the car looked like a Jeep.

It only took a few seconds behind the wheel, however, to realize that this was a substantially improved Mustang (despite the somewhat disappointing horsepower). Handling, ergonomics, comfort, and drivability were all far superior to the car it replaced; noise, vibration, and harshness were dramatically reduced. The only aspects in which the older cars were better were straight-line acceleration and storage. The new car was indeed heavier, and the 5-liter engine seemed noticeably less torquey. Quarter-mile times were definitely a few ticks off. *Muscle Mustangs & Fast Fords* got a five-speed GT with 3.08

Ford played off the Mustang's heritage in a variety of ways on its new car. The galloping horse emblem on the open grille (left) was one of the more obvious. All coupes (bottom) came with a trunk; the hatchback was deemed expendable because engineers thought it compromised structural integrity. Opposite: Midway through the 1994 model year, Ford introduced its newest Cobra, both in coupe and for the first time since 1970, as a convertible. All convertibles were Indy Pace Car replicas—yes, the Cobra paced the big one in '94.

1995 COBRA R: RACING INTO HISTORY

When it built the 1993 Cobra R model, Ford learned some valuable lessons about road racing. Yes, the '93 Cobra R handled fabulously, but it got out-horsepowered by the competition and couldn't go nearly as far on a tank of fuel (only 15.4 gallons). Also, by producing only 107 '93 R models, few ever turned a lap in competition; instead, they were snapped up by collectors and speculators.

Not only was Ford paying attention to these lessons, it actually did something about them. First, it replaced the standard gas tank with a race-legal 20-gallon fuel cell. Then it more than doubled production, building a total of 252 cars, 250 of which were sold to the general public. To purchase one, you had to show a competition license from a sanctioned racing body.

As for horsepower, Ford installed a GT-40-ized version of its 351 marine engine that was rated at 300 hp and 365 foot-pounds of torque. A fiberglass cowl-induction hood was employed, both to help offset the weight of the larger engine and to provide clearance for the intake manifold. A heavy-duty Tremec 3550 five-speed transmission backed up the 5.8L mill.

To improve its handling, expensive Koni shocks and struts were installed at all four corners, and progressive-rate Eibach coil springs kept the body off the tires. Speaking of which, BFGoodrich Comp T/A radials (P255/45ZR17) rode on luscious five-spoke A-Mold aluminum wheels.

In street trim (it was sold as a fifty-state emissions-legal automobile), the Cobra R was capable of 13.50-second elapsed times on street tires. With slicks, they ran in the 12.9s at nearly 106 mph.

The Cobra Rs did decently in competition, considering that they were built just before the season started and teams didn't have enough development time. They didn't win any road races in 1995, but that changed in 1996, when the Steeda Autosports team found itself in the winner's circle on more than one occasion. They won two IMSA races and missed winning the championship by only one point to Pontiac.

The 1995 Cobra R had all the ingredients to set a Mustang lover's pulse racing, including a 300-horse 5.8L engine, a fiberglass cowl-induction hood, 20-gallon fuel cell, and special tires, wheels, and suspension. The V6 Mustang seats were used to save weight (and money) and, again, the rear seat and radio were deleted.

Ford introduced the new Mustang with almost as much fanfare as the original nearly thirty years before. Working in conjunction with Mustang clubs, it previewed the car in 100 key cities nationwide weeks before they went on sale. Los Angeles, Chicago, and New York (at the site of the original World's Fair in Flushing) hosted Mustang gatherings, as did a number of other cities.

How was the new Mustang greeted by the automotive press? Warmly, but in head-to-head comparisons with the Camaro and Firebird, it fared poorly. Even though it out-sold those two cars combined, journalists were not impressed with its long list of virtues. It did win the Motor Trend Car of the Year award, but so did the Renault Alliance and Chevy Vega at one time or another.

SNAKES ALIVE!

If the ordinary 1994 Mustang GT was not enough to get enthusiasts' blood boiling, Ford's Special Vehicle Team satiated their desire with a limited run of Cobra Mustangs. Like their 1993 predecessors, the new Cobras offered a host of honest-to-goodness virtues for not much more cash. A cast-version of the after-market GT-40 intake and GT-40 cylinder heads lay under the hood, as did a larger throttle body (among other things), which brought horsepower up from 215 to 240. The suspension was softened with linear rate springs from the V6 model, while different shocks and sway bars helped the car hold the road better.

A set of 17-inch Goodyear GS-C asymmetric tires on gorgeous five-slot wheels replaced the standard 16-inch and optional 17-inch tires of the GT. Up front, giant PBR brake calipers helped slow the Cobra from speed. Inside, white-faced gauges replaced the black-with-white numerals, with a 160-mph speedometer supplanting the GT's 150-mph unit.

The front fascia differed from the GT in that there were round fog lights instead of rectangular ones. Out back, the Cobra carried a different wing on its deck lid from that of the GT.

As a road car, the new Cobra was a gem. Its compliant suspension coddled drivers, yet still offered excellent control. While some complained that it was too soft on the racetrack, this isn't the market that the Cobra was

gears to turn a credible 14.45 at 94 mph—comparable with earlier GTs—but gone was the budget-racer's dream machine, the inexpensive LX.

And gone, too, in the transition was the old hatchback model. The '94 was offered only as a coupe or a convertible, and while the former had plenty of space with the rear seats folded down, it was extremely difficult to load through the narrow trunk opening. Ford claimed that it couldn't produce a hatchback with sufficient structural integrity, a rather lame excuse given that the Japanese were exporting such hatchbacks at two-thirds the cost of the Mustang.

Opposite: This '95 Mustang GT is equipped with the optional 17-inch wheels and tires, a $380 option. Above: Color choices for the 1996 Cobra were black, laser red metallic, white, and "Mystic," a custom (and limited-edition) three-step paint process that changed color from black to green to maroon and various combinations thereof as light reflected off it. Left: The quad-cam 4.6L 4-valve made 305 horsepower and revved easily to where stock 5-liters feared to tread. Following page: To cut costs on the '96 Cobra, the standard GT rear wing was now used. Laser red metallic replaced Rio red the same year, to the disappointment of some Cobraphiles.

SALEEN MUSTANGS—FACTORY-AUTHORIZED TERRORS

Back when the first Mustangs rolled off the assembly line, Carroll Shelby worked his magic on them and thus, a legend was born. The Shelby GT350 (and later GT500s) would become forces both in road racing and at the burger stand. Today, they are highly prized by collectors, selling for many times their original value.

Fast forward to 1984. Successful southern-California road racer Steve Saleen, who had raced Shelby GT350s, came up with the idea to build an upscale, track-inspired, limited-edition Mustang to be sold exclusively through select Ford dealerships. He pitched his idea to Lee Morse of Ford Special Vehicle Operations and sold him on it.

Legend has it that Saleen took his sister's '84 Mustang and added his "Racecraft" suspension (lowering springs, Bilstein gas struts and shocks, chassis stiffeners, polyurethane sway-bar bushings), plus alloy wheels and P215/60HR Goodyear Eagle GT tires. To keep the Saleen from looking like every other Mustang on the road, the car wore special side skirts, a different front air dam and rear spoiler, and unique Saleen graphics on the sides.

Under the hood, things were virtually unchanged. This kept Saleen from having to recertify the car for the federal government. Over the next few years, Saleen added dealers across the country and sold thousands of cars in the process. On the racetracks, this hybrid enjoyed remarkable success, winning the SCCA Escort Endurance Series world championship in 1987.

When the '94 Mustang was introduced with many of the Saleen improvements, like five-lug wheels, four-wheel disc brakes, and stiffer chassis standard, the Saleen automobile company regrouped and once again offered the public a vastly improved package. Dubbed the S-351, it was huge step toward making the Mustang a world-class GT. Aside from a lower stance, reworked suspension, 18-inch wheels and tires, and a killer body kit and graphics package, the '94 Saleen Mustangs were noteworthy for one thing: they were powered by a 372-horsepower version of the much-sought-after 351 Windsor V8. Enhancements came from Edelbrock aluminum cylinder heads, an optional supercharger, and a special intake package.

For 1996, the package was refined further with new cylinder heads, a different camshaft, and a host of other changes, which boosted horsepower output to 400. (A supercharger, which boosted output to 500 pavement-shredding ponies, was optional for a few thousand more.)

This writer had the opportunity to perform a battery of tests on a naturally aspirated S-351 in southern California. It handled the Angeles Crest Freeway with aplomb, exploded through traffic, and ripped off 13-second elapsed times at the drag strip (12.40 on special drag-racing slicks at 109.98 mph). On a lonely stretch of desert, it pulled all the way to 165 mph, though the optimistic 200-mph speedometer indicated 180.

Testing a supercharged S-351, *Muscle Mustangs & Fast Fords* blistered the quarter mile at California's Carlsbad Raceway in 11.33 seconds at 122 mph. Top speed was reported to be 177 mph. Truly, the Saleen Mustangs were not for the faint of heart. They were (and are) pricey (starting at $35,000) but are a special breed of horse.

Steve Saleen made his name as a championship race driver in Mustangs in the 1980s. Just as Carroll Shelby did in the sixties, he parlayed that success into building specially modified Saleen Mustangs that were available as new cars with a full Ford factory warranty. At right, the '94 Saleen SR at Charlotte Motor Speedway in North Carolina.

removed more 5-liter V8s from inventory. This would be important, as 1995 marked the end of the line for the dependable, popular, and powerful small-block Ford V8.

1996 AND BEYOND

After thirty years of duty in the Mustang platform, the small-block V8 was finally replaced in 1996 with a pair of new high-tech 4.6L V8 engines. The first, a single-overhead-cam design, had a cast-iron block with aluminum heads, a composite-intake manifold, and stainless steel exhaust manifolds. In less powerful trim, it had been used since 1992 in Crown Victorias, Lincoln Continental Town Cars, Thunderbirds, and Cougars. In Mustang trim, it made 215 horsepower, exactly the same as the '94–'95 5.0, but is far less torquey.

For those seeking more performance, Ford offered a new Cobra, powered by a 305-horse variation of the Lincoln Mark VIII's dual-overhead-cam, four-valve-per-cylinder, all-aluminum engine. Changes in the camshafts, intake manifold, and other areas accounted for the 25-horsepower difference between the Cobra and Lincoln versions. Installed in the car, the 4.6L DOHC is an amazing power plant. Quarter-mile distances can be covered in under 14 seconds at 100 mph, with the top speed coming in at about 154 mph. It's a real thoroughbred.

A limited number (2,000) of '96 Cobras were scheduled to be built with the "Mystic" paint option. Black is the only true pigment in the paint, so as light reflects off the car, the color changes to purple, green, gold, and black.

It's hard to say where the Mustang is charging as we enter the twenty-first century. An independent rear suspension is fast becoming a reality as is another 5.8L Cobra R. There's also talk of a 5.4L version of the modular truck engine being fitted with high flow two-valve-per-cylinder head and other performance hardware. There may be a supercharger or even five-valve-per-cylinder heads.

At this writing, though, it's all conjecture. The only people who know where the Mustang is going are the folks from Ford, and they're not talking. One thing is certain: Ford will continue to offer V8 power in a rear-drive, relatively inexpensive platform. This formula has worked for more than thirty years, wooing millions of buyers. You can't argue with that kind of success.

Above: The single-overhead cam 4.6L V8 engine replaced the venerable 5-liter in the Mustang GT in 1996. While smoother than the 5.0, it doesn't offer nearly as much torque.

Opposite: All '94 and newer Mustangs except the '95 R model have an unusually high ride height from the factory (check out the amount of space between the tops of the tires and the wheelwells). This has prompted many Mustang owners to install lowering springs.

built for. At the track, it was capable of high 13-second quarter-mile times, certainly comparable with many of the most powerful Mustangs.

To help celebrate the new Mustang, it was picked to serve as the pace car for the 1994 Indianapolis 500. But it wasn't a GT model. No, Ford made the most of this opportunity by building Mustang Cobra convertibles to handle the chores at Indy.

The year 1995 saw few changes to the Mustang lineup. Sales were still brisk, but some longtime fans thought the price of the GT was too high, that there were too many frills keeping the 215 from performing its duty as rapidly as it could. Responding to the call of enthusiasts, Ford introduced the Mustang GTS. Devoid of frills like power driver's seat, power windows, fog lights, and a rear wing, the GTS offered a more reasonable price tag than the GT and a slightly better performance, thanks to its lighter weight. The GTS came with a V6 Mustang interior, base seats, plastic steering wheel, and 16-inch wheels. Few came with air conditioning, though it was available. The GTS pleased hard-core Mustang enthusiasts and

Mustang Clubs

National and International

Vintage Mustang Owners Association
P.O. Box 5772
San Jose, CA 95150-5772

The Mustang Club of America, Inc.
3588 Highway 138, Suite 365
Stockbridge, GA 30281

Gateway 5.0 Mustang Club, Inc.
636 Oregon Trail Ct.
St. Charles, MO 63304-7984

Cobra Owners Club of America
22365 El Toro Rd., Suite 239
Lake Forest, CA 92630

SVO Owners Association
4222 I-75 Business Spur, Suite 429
Sault Ste. Marie, MI 49783

Shelby American Automobile Club
P.O. Box 788
Sharon, CT 06069-0788

Regional

Birmingham Mustang Club
36777 Guyton Rd.
Hoover, AL 35244

Heart of Dixie Mustang Club
P.O. Box 3594
Montgomery, AL 36109

North Alabama Late Model Mustang
   Club
917 Weatherly Rd.
Huntsville, AL 35803

Copperstate Mustang Club, Inc.
P.O. Box 31249
Phoenix, AZ 85046

Old Pueblo Mustang Club
10041 Rau Ann Place
Tucson, AZ 85749

Southern Arizona Mustang Club
P.O. Box 44145
Tucson, AZ 85733

Central Arkansas Mustangers
2900 Spring St.
Hot Springs, AR 71901

Northwest Arkansas Mustang Club
P.O. Box 254
Springdale, AR 72762

Southern Arkansas Mustangs
6020 Sherwood Ln.
El Dorado, AR 71730

Bay Area Mustang Association
P.O. Box 3043
Hayward, CA 94544

Mustang Club of Southern California
P.O. Box 1451
Upland, CA 91785

Mustang Owners Club of California
P.O. Box 8261
Van Nuys, CA 91409-8261

Orange County Mustang Club
P.O. Box 1013
Cypress, CA 90630

Denver Mustang Club
5682 S. Robb St.
Littleton, CO 80127

The Early Mustang Club of Colorado
11103 West 67th Way
Arvada, CO 80004

High Country Mustang Club
1441 Melissa Dr.
Loveland, CO 80537

Blue Oval Mustang Shelby Club
P.O. Box 4533
Danbury, CT 06813-4553

Lower Delaware Mustang Club
Rt. 1, Box 47AA
Seaford, DE 19973

Imperial Mustangs of Polk County
5098 Varty Rd.
Winter Haven, FL 33884

Mustang Club of West Central Florida
P.O. Box 271
Oneco, FL 34264

Southwest Florida Mustang Club
3101 Terrace Ave.
Naples, FL 33942

Heart of Georgia Mustang Club
P.O. Box 8404
Warner Robins, GA 31095

Savannah Mustang Club
P.O. Box 13204
Savannah, GA 31406

Tara Mustang Club
P.O. Box 1494
Fayetteville, GA 30214

Aloha Mustang and Shelby Club of
   Hawaii
P.O. Box 6216
Honolulu, HI 96818

Treasure Valley Mustang Club
P.O. Box 556
Boise, ID 83701

Central Illinois Mustangers
61 Ronald Dr.
Decatur, IL 62526

Southern Illinois Mustang Association
481 Valley Dr.
E. Alton, IL 62024

Stallions Gate Mustang Club
5348 W. Byron, #2
Chicago, IL 60641

Eastern Iowa Mustangs
P.O. Box 352
117 Third Ave. West
Alburnett, IA 52202

Mustang Club of Central Iowa
P.O. Box 8383
Des Moines, IA 50301

Southern Iowa Mustang Club
114 East 12th St.
Pella, IA 50219

Mid-Kansas Mustang and Ford
   Powered Club
P.O. Box 101
Inman, KS 67546

South Central Kansas Mustang Club
P.O. Box 161081
Wichita, KS 67216-1081

Vintage Mustang Club of Kansas City
P.O. Box 40082
Overland Park, KS 66204

Western Kansas Mustang Club
1344 Federal
Hays, KS 67601

Bluegrass Mustang Club
P.O. Box 11732
Lexington, KY 40577-1732

South Central Kansas Mustang Club
P.O. Box 429
Buckner, KY 40010

Baton Rouge Mustang Club
12222 Louis White Rd.
Geismar, LA 70734

Classic Mustang Association
205 Wiegand Dr.
Bridge City, LA 70094

Red River Classic Mustang Club
P.O. Box 2096
Shreveport, LA 71166-2096

Mustang Club of Maryland
1206 Bartus Ct.
Belair, MD 21014

Mustang Club of Western Maryland
P.O. Box 1302
Frederick, MD 21702

Cape Cod Mustang Club
P.O. Box 1352
Marstons Mills, MA 02648

Mustang and Classic Ford Club of New
   England
P.O. Box 963
North Attleboro, MA 02761

Mustang Owners Club of S.E. Michigan
P.O. Box 39088
Redford, MI 48239

Mid-Michigan Mustangs
P.O. Box 0054
Battle Creek, MI 49016-0054

Upper Peninsula Mustangs
1289 M28
Marquette, MI 49844

West Michigan Mustang Club
4264 Arbortown Dr.
Grandville, MI 49418

Hiawatha Mustang Club
807 W. Park St.
Cannon Falls, MN 55009

Mississippi Coast Mustang Club, Inc.
136 Watersedge Dr.
Ocean Springs, MS 39564-5123

North Mississippi Mustang Club
P.O. Box 404
Southaven, MS 38671

Central Missouri Mustang Club
P.O. Box 513
Jefferson City, MO 65102

Mineral Area Mustang Club
P.O. Box 114
Park Hills, MO 63601

Show-Me Mustang Club
P.O. Box 137
Hazelwood, MO 63042

Bridger Mountain Pony Car Club
1507 Wildflower Way
Bozeman, MT 59715

Last Chance Mustang and Specialty
   Ford Club
1420 Sorenson Rd.
Helena, MT 59601

Treasure State Mustang Club
4400 7th Ave. South
Great Falls, MT 59405

Capitol City Ford/Mustang Club
841 W. Rose
Lincoln, NE 68522

Mustang Car Club of Omaha
P.O. Box 6565
Omaha, NE 68106

Platte Valley Mustangs
2104 24th St.
Columbus, NE 68601

Mustang Club of Las Vegas
P.O. Box 28705
Las Vegas, NV 89126-2705

Reno Mustang Car Club
P.O. Box 12453
Reno, NV 89510-2453

New Hampshire Mustang Club
71 McAllister Rd.
Bedford, NH 03110

Garden State Regional Mustang Club
P.O. Box 193
Woodridge, NJ 07075

North Jersey Mustang, Inc.
P.O. Box 110015
Nutley, NJ 07110

West Jersey Mustang/Ford
    Performance Club
P.O. Box 504
Annadale, NJ 08801

First Pennsylvania Mustang Club
6 Tainter St.
Box 213
Peapack, NJ 07977

Rio Grande Mustang of New Mexico,
    Inc.
13825 Cedarbrook Ave. NE
Albuquerque, NM 87111

Hudson Valley Mustang Association,
    Ltd.
P.O. Box 1283
Wappingers Falls, NY 12590

Long Island Mustang/Shelby Club
8003 Myrtle Ave.
Glendale, NY 11385

Shelby Mustang of Rochester, Inc.
P.O. Box 93356
Rochester, NY 14692

Syracuse Shelby Mustang Club, Inc.
5108 Cpl. Welch Rd.
Syracuse, NY 13215

Club Mustang
1923 Lejeune Blvd.
Jacksonville, NC 28540

Gate City Triad Mustang Club
1905 Gillespie St.
Fayetteville, NC 28306

Southeastern North Carolina Mustang
    Club
495 Rivenbarktown Rd.
Wallace, NC 28466

Tarheel Mustang Club
410 Holly Hill Rd.
Murfreesboro, NC 27855

Dakota Super Fords
RR 1, Box 2
Rugby, ND 58368

Classic Mustang Club of Ohio
1233 Colston Dr.
Westerville, OH 43081

Mid-Ohio Valley Mustang Club
980 George St.
Blepre, OH 45714

Tri-State Mustang-FoMoCo Club
5861 Dry Ridge Rd.
Cincinnati, OH 45252

Northeastern Ohio Mustang Club
3636 Risher Rd.
Youngstown, OH 44511

Arkansas Valley Mustang Club
Rt. 5, Box 796
Muldrow, OK 74948

Green County Classic Mustangs
P.O. Box 471361
Tulsa, OK 74147-1361

Oklahoma Mustang Club
415 W. Greenwood Dr.
Mustang, OK 73064

Mid Coast Mustang Club
P.O. Box 615
Scottsburg, OR 97473

Mustang Wranglers of Oregon
P.O. Box 372
Hillsboro, OR 97123

Capitol Area Mustang Club of Oregon
P.O. Box 4004
Salem, OR 97302

Rogue Mustangs and Classic Fords
P.O. Box 8393
Medford, OR 97501

Greater Pittsburgh Mustang Club
208 Wallingford Dr.
Pittsburgh, PA 15237

Lake Erie Mustang Owners Club
P.O. Box 8602
Erie, PA 16505

North Central Mustang Club
1950 East Third St.
Williamsport, PA 17701

Valley Forge Mustang Club
322 Colonial Dr.
Exton, PA 19341

Foothills Mustang Club
103 Essex Ct.
Greenwood, SC 29649-9561

Rapid Mustang Club of the Black Hills
P.O. Box 1649
Rapid City, SD 57709

Mustangs of Memphis
4968 Chuck
Memphis, TN 38118

Tennessee Valley Mustang Club
P.O. Box 5294
Oak Ridge, TN 37831-5294

Lubbock Mustang Club
P.O. Box 6154
Lubbock, TX 79493-6154

Coastal Bend Mustang Club
7121 South Padre Island Dr., Suite 302
Corpus Christi, TX 78404

Mustang Club of Houston
P.O. Box 14114
Humble, TX 77347

North Texas Mustang Club
P.O. Box 531374
Grand Prairie, TX 75053

Shelby Cobra Association of Texas
7809 Ivy Lane
Rowlett, TX 75088

Texoma Mustang Club
P.O. Box 1223
Gainesville, TX 76241

Shelby/Mustang Club of Utah
11075 S. Mary Dr.
Sandy, UT 84092

Lynchburg Area Mustang Club
P.O. Box 11843
Lynchburg, VA 24506

Mustang Club of Tidewater
330 West Brambleton Ave., #1012
Norfolk, VA 23510

National Capital Region Mustang Club
9307 Shouse Dr.
Vienna, VA 22182

Southeastern Virginia Mustang Club
c/o Freedom Ford
7520 Military Highway
Norfolk, VA 23518

Island Classic Mustang Club
P.O. Box 2628
Oak Harbor, WA 98277

Mustangs Northwest
14023 Bear Creek Rd.
Woodinville, WA 98072

Mustangs Unlimited
P.O. Box 84118
Vancouver, WA 98684-0118

Pacific Northwest Mustang Club
P.O. Box 1693
Richland, WA 99357

Sun Country Mustang Club
P.O. Box 556
Moxee, WA 98936

Pierce Country Mustang Club
P.O. Box 445
Tacoma, WA 98401-0445

Mustang Club of West Virginia
1702 Massey Circle
South Charles, WV 25303

Shenandoah Valley Mustang Club
Rt. 3, Box 422
Harpers Ferry, WV 25425

Badgerland Mustang Club
P.O. Box 338
Poynette, WI 53955

Fox Valley Mustang Club
2309 N. Idlewild Ct.
Green Bay, WI 54303

Madison Area Mustang Association
8 North Franklin St.
Madison, WI 53703

The Wisconsin Early Mustangers
2511 W. Carrington Ave.
Oak Creek, WI 53154

Big Horn Basin Mustang Association
2205 Berdahl Ave.
Cody, WY 82414

Montreal Mustang
830 Blvd. Provencher
Case postale 86033 Postal Sq.
Brossard, Quebec
J4W 1YO

Nova Scotia Mustang Club
16 Lantana Terrace
Dartmouth, NS
B2X 3L2

INDEX

A

Acceleration, 21, 80, 92
Airbag, 97
Air conditioning, 16, 29
American Motors
    AMX, 41
    Javelin, 41, 51, 60–61
AMX, 41
Ash, Davc, 17

B

Barr, Bill, 38, 45, 48
Barracuda, 19, 21, 25, 33, 38, 60
BMW 3 series, 90
Bordinat, Eugene, 17, 50
Boss 302, 45, *46–47*, 48–49, 50, 53, 55, 59
Boss 351, *58*, 59
Boss 429, 49, 50, *50–51*, 51, 53, 55, 69
Brakes, 20
Bucket seats, 14, 16, 17, 38
Bucknum, Ronnie, 60
Buick
    LeSabre, 82
    Regal, 82

C

California Highway Patrol, 83
California Special, 37
Camaro, 25, 26, *28*, 33, 38, 45, 51, 56, 60, 69, 80, 83, 99, 101, 102
Capri, 66, 68, 76, *76*, 80, 90
Car Craft, 71, 76
Car and Driver, 19, 21, 53, 56, 59, 83
Car Life, 29, 33, 45
Cars Illustrated, 92
Central Fuel Injection, 83
Charlie's Angels, 70

Chevrolet
    Camaro, 25, 26, *28*, 33, 38, 45, 51, 56, 60, 80, 83, 99, 101, 102
    Corvair, 14, *14*, 19, 21, 25, 48, 51, 60
    Corvette, 12, *12*, 13, 20, 48, 50, 104
    Monte Carlo, 69, 82
Chrysler
    Hemihead engine, 49
    LcBaron, 74
Cobra, 20, *96*, 97, 99, 101, 104, *105*, *109*, 115
    R models, 99, *99*, 106, *106–107*, 115
Cobra II, 70, *70*, 73, *73*
Cobra Jet, 33, 38, *41*, *49*, 58–59, 61, 69
Compact cars, 14, 66, 68, *68*,
Console, 30
Convertible, *59*, 68–69
    1967, *29*, 29
    1973, 62
    1983, 74, *75*, 83
    1993, *98*
    1994, 109
    LX, 97
    SAAC MK 2, 92
Corvair, 14, *14*, 21, 48, 51, 60
Corvair Monza, 14, 19, 25
Corvette, 12, *12*, 13, 20, 48, 50, 104
Cougar, 25, 26, *28*, 38, 41, 51, 60, 69, 115
Crown Victoria, 101, 115

D

Datsun 240Z, 66
Dealer Special Orders (DSO), 101
DeLorean, John Z., 26
Deluxe Decor Group, 45
Dodge
    Challenger, 56
    Dart, 60
    Lancer, 14

Donohue, Mark, 49, 60
Drag Pack, 55, 61
Drag-strip gears, 21

E

Edsel, 15
Exterior Decor Group, 29

F

Fairlane Committee, 15
Fairmont, 74, 76, *76*, 77
Falcon, 8, 14, 19, 74
Fastback, 10, *11*, 19, 21, 24, 25, *25*, 29, 33, *34–35*
Fengler, Harlan, *15*
Fiberglass technology, 12
Firebird, 26, *28*, 33, 38, 51, 56, 69, 102
Fog lights, *30*, 31, 37, 80
Follmer, George, 60, 61
Ford, Henry II, 24, 48, 50
Ford. *See also* Mustang.
    Edsel, 15
    Fairmont, 74, 76, *76*, 77
    Falcon, 8, 14, 19, 74
    Maverick, *68*, 70
    Pinto, 68, 70
    Taurus, 10
    Thunderbird, 12–13, 69, 115
    Torino, 49
    V8 engine, 12
Four-cylinder engine, 18, 82, *82*, 88, 89
"Four on the floor"-style transmissions, 17
Fox-4 platform, 74, 76
Foyt, A.J., 15
Fuel-injection system, 89, 92

G

Ghia model, 66, *67*, 69
Grande, 42, *44*, 45

Grand Prix, 69, 82
Grey, Lee, 37
GT , 80, 83, 86, 90, *91*, 92, 101, 102, 104, *108*, 109, 115
GT 350, 20–21, *20*, 31, 52, 53, 70, 112
GT 500, 9, *29*, 31, *31*, 52, *53*, *54*, 55, 112
GT/California Special Recognition Guide, 37
GT/CS, 37
GT Equipment Group, 24
GTS, 115
Gurney, Dan, 60

H

Handling, 30, 45, 69, 76, 80
Hatchback, 86, *87*, 92, *93*, 104, 109
Headlights, 31, 48, *48*, 53, 69, 77, 90
High Country Special, *36*, 37 *37*,
Hot Rod, 10, 33, 38, 71, 76–77

I

Iacocca, Lee, 14–15, 24, 48, 62, 66
Indianapolis 500 pace car, *15*, 78, *79*, 115
Instrument panel, 24, 29, 30, 90, 104
Interior Decor Group, 24, 29–30

J

Javelin, 41, 51
Jeep, 69
Jetfire, 82
Jones, Parnelli, 60

K

Kar Kraft, 51
King Cobra, 71, *71*, 76
Kirschenbaum, Al, 92
Knudsen, Semon E. "Bunkie," 48, 50

L

Lancer, 14
LeSabre, 82
Leslie, Ed, 60
Limited Production Options (LPO),
    101
Lincoln
    Continental Town Car, 115
    Mark VIII, 102, 115
Little Red, 37
LX, 90, 92, *93*, 97, 99, 101, 109

M

Mach 1, 9, *44*, 45, 48, 58, *64–65*, 69
Mach III, *101*, 104
Maverick, *68*, 70
Mazda, 97
McHose, Chuck, 31
Mercury
    Capri, 66, 68, 76, *76*, 80, 90
    Cougar, 25, 26, *28*, 38, 41, 51,
        60, 69, 115
    Cyclone, 49
    Zephyr, 74, *76*, 77
Monte Carlo, 69, 82
Monza, 14, 19, 25
Monza Spyder, 14, 19
Moore, Bud, 60, 61
Morrison, Jim, 8
Morse, Lee, 112
Motor Trend, 29, 33, 45, 80
MuscleCars, 99, 101
Muscle Mustangs & Fast Fords, 9,
        99, 101, 104, 109, 112
Mustang. *See also* Mustang I and
        Mustang II.
    1965, 10, *11*, *14*, 16, *16–17*, 19,
        19, 24, 68
    1966, 21, *22–23*, 25, *25*
    1967, 26, *27*, 28–33, *30*, *31*
    1968, *30*, *32*, 33, *36*, 37, 38, *39*,
        41
    1969, 42, *43*, *44*, 45, *46–47*,
        48–49

1970, 53, 55
1971, 56, *57*, 58–59, 61–62
1972, 62
1973, *59*, *61*, 62, *63*
1974, 66, *67*, 68–69, *68*
1976, 69–70
1977, *69*, 73
1978, 73, *73*
1979, 76–77, *77*, 78, *79*, 80
1980, 82
1981, 80
1982, 80, *80*, *81*, 83
1983, 74, *75*, 82, 83, *83*,
1984, 83, *84–85*, 86, *87*, 112
1985, 89
1986, 82, 89, *89*
1987, 90, *91*, 92
1988, 97
1989, 92, *94–95*
1990, 97
1993, *96*, 97, *98*, 104, 106
1994, 15, 102, *103*, 104, *105*,
        109, 112, *113*, *114*, 115,
        116–117
1995, 106, *106-107*, *108*, 109,
        115
1996, 109, *110–111*, 112
clubs, 8–9, 116–117
competition to, 27, *28*, 33, 38, 41
coupe, 19, *29*, 42, *44*, 45, 60, 69,
        77, *104*, 109
experimental cars, 18, *18*
fastback, 10, *11*, 19, 21, 24, 25,
        25, 29, 33, *34-35*, 42
hatchback, 77, 80, 86, *87*, 92,
        93, 104, 109
introduction of, 10–19
marketing of, *21*, *77*
market research for, 14–15, 17
options for, 8, 12, 19, 24–25, 101
as pace car, *15*, 78, *79*, 115
price of, 8, 59, 83, 92
sales of, 24, 25, 38, 41, 45, 51,
        62, 77, 92, 97

styling of, 17, 24–25, 29, 38, 42,
        56, 77, 80, 83, 90, 104
    third-generation, 74, 76
    turbocharged, 82, *82*, 83
Mustang I, 18, *18*
Mustang II
    Cobra II, 70, *70*, 73, *73*
    color scheme, *69*, 70
    drawbacks of, 74
    Ghia, 66, *67*, 69
    introduction of, 62, 66, 68
    King Cobra, 71, *71*, *72*, 73, 76
    sales of, 69, 70
    Stallion, 70
    styling of, 68–69, 73
Mustang II show car, 18, *18*

N

Nader, Ralph, 14
NASCAR stock-car racing, 12, 49, 51
National Hot Rod Association, 38
Newitt, Paul M., 37
New York World's Fair, 10
Nicholson, Don, 71, 76

O

Oil embargo, 55, 66
Oldsmobile Jetfire, 82
OPEC, 55, 66, 74
Oros, Joseph, 17
Overhead-cam (OHC), 68

P

Pace Car, 15, 78, *79*, 115
Penske, Roger, 49, 60
Pinto, 68, 70
Plymouth
    Barracuda, 19, 21, 25, 26, 33,
        38, 51, 60
    Valiant, 14
Police pursuit vehicle, 100–101, *100*
Pontiac

Firebird, 26, *28*, 33, 38, 51, 56,
        69, 102
    Grand Prix, 69, 82
    Trans Am, 69, 70, 73, 82, 90
Pony interior, 24
Porsche 930, 82

Q

Quadra-Shock suspension, 83

R

Rack-and-pinion steering, 18, 69, 77
Regal, 82
Revson, Peter, 60
Roger Penske z/28, 49
Roush, Jack, 78

S

S-351, 112
SAAC
    MK 1, 92, *93*
    MK 2, 92
    Snake, 92
Saleen, Steve, 112, *112*
Saleen Mustang, 112, *113*
SCCA Escort Endurance Series,
        112
Seat belts, 24, 74
Shelby, Carroll, 20, *20*, 31, 52, 60,
        112
Shelby American Automobile Club,
        92
Shelby Mustangs, 9, 20–21, *20*, 31,
        31, 42, 52–53, *52–53*, *54*,
        55, 70
Shinoda, Larry, 45, 48, 50, *51*, 53, 56
Shinoda Design Associates, 50
Sinatra, Frank, 8
Sonny and Cher, 8
Special Handling Package, 24
Special Service Package, 83,
        100–101, *100*

Special Vehicle Operations, 83, 88, 112

Special Vehicle Team, 99

Speedometer, 24, 61, 97

Sports Car Club of America (SCCA), 20, 45, 60, 112

Sports Car Graphic, 56

SportsRoof, 42, 45, 53, 56

Sprint, 62

Stacey, Pete, 31

Stallion, 70

Steeda Autosports team, 106

Steering wheel, 18, 21, 30, 38, 61–62, *62*, 86, 97

Stripes, 9, 73

Super Stock & Drag Illustrated, 92

Suspension, 18, 19, 30, 45, 69, 76, 80, 83, 86

SVO, 83, *84–85*, 86, 88–89, *88*, 90

T

Tachometer, 69

Taillights, 18, 29, 33, 53, 69, 90

Taurus, 10

Thompson, Dick, 60

Thunderbird, 12–13, *13*, 14, 69, 115

Tires, 45, 76, 86, 89, 99, 106, 109

Titus, Jerry, 60

Toyota Celica, 66

Trans Am, 69, 70, 73, 82, 90

Trans-Am competition, 49, 60–61, *61*

T-roof, *83*, 83, 97

TRX handling/suspension package, 76, 80, 83, 86

Tullius, Bob, 60

Turbocharger, 82, *82*, 89

U

Unsafe at Any Speed (Nader), 14

V

V4 engine, 12, 18, 82, *82*, 89

V6 engine, 12, 24, 62, 68, 69, 70, 76, 82

V8 engine, 10, 86, 89
  302, 48–49, *48*, 69, 70, 71, 78, 80
  351 Windsor, 112
  429, 51
  4.6-liter, 102, *109*, 115, *115*
  5-liter, 90, 92, 99, 101, 102, 104
  big-block, 28, 30, *30*, 33, 62
  Challenger, 24, *24*
  Cleveland, 53, 59, 61
  Cobra Jet, 45, 61, 62
  horsepower, 25, 80, 82, 83
  small-block, 17
  Thunderbird Special, 33
  turbocharged, 82
  Y-block, 12, 13

V8 Mustang Specifications Guide, 92

Valiant, 14

Volkswagen Beetle, 14

W

Watkins Glen, New York, 18

Wheel
  base, 28, 56, 77
  turbine, 92, *94–95*

Y

Yarborough, Cale, 60

Yarbrough, LeeRoy, 60

Y-block V8 engine, 12, 13

Z

Zephyr, 74, *76*, 77

PHOTOGRAPHY CREDITS